D1607022

Indian Slow Cooker Cookbook

Top 100 Indian Slow Cooker Recipes from Restaurant Classics to Innovative Modern Indian Recipes All Easily Made At Home in a Slow Cooker

By: Myra Gupta

Want to kick it up a notch?

Double down on healthy living with a full week of fresh, healthy fruit and vegetable juice recipes. A new juice for every day of the week!

Grab this bonus recipe eBook *free* as our gift to you:

http://juice7.hotbooks.org

Legal notice

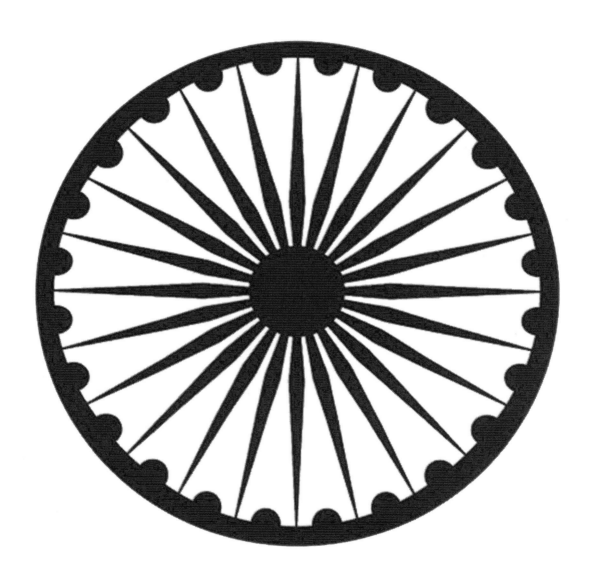

Contents

Introduction

As one of the oldest civilizations still in existence, India contains over a billion people. They are spread out over a diverse set of regions, religions, languages, and even clothing choices. However, this mixture comes together to create the whole of India. Just as the country is varied, so is the food that you can find in the country. Sometimes it's defined by the region as there are some different crops that you will find it specific spots. Sometimes it will depend on the major religion of the area. People that have been in India have also changed the food that they eat as well.

Indian cuisine is loved around the world because of the variety of spices that it uses. Of course, the cuisine is still changing and evolving. The food has become more and more popular which means that the flavors aren't as foreign as they were once before. Dishes like Garam Masala and Haldi are making appearances in kitchens everywhere.

But even as people are falling in love with Indian food, people are running into another issue: time. These dishes are harder to prepare when you are up against the fast moving pace of the rest of your life. People want to still make good food for their family, but it has to be able to work with their life. Many dishes require much more time and attention than we have to give to the dishes we want to make.

In order to help you, we're going to focus on the Dum pukht method of cooking. It is a slow cooking process. It means that you'll be cooking some food in its own juices. It uses fewer spices but keeps the flavors interesting. And these are dishes that you'll be able to put together and then go off and do everything that you need to do. You'll come home to a house that not only smells great but has a dish ready for you already.

Indian Cooking Basics

Everything about an Indian kitchen is wonderful. The spices and sweetness that mix there are incredibly unique and powerful in the modern world. Just the aroma of the spices will make your mouth water. The dish will be even better than the smell. Because of all the flavors and how they mix together, a lot of people have fallen in love with Indian cuisine. While some dishes might seem like they're beyond you, the dishes we are going to go over in this book are going to be well within the range of things that you can do.

Important Techniques

While the common perception is that Indian cuisine and the associated cooking styles are complicated, you'll find that there are some very not complicated techniques that will allow you to get to those complicated flavors. However, regardless of the complicated nature of the dish, there are some basics that you will need to know.

This recipe book is focused on the slow cooker recipes that you are going to be using, but there are still techniques that are going to be important to you. We're breaking them down here because you might face several of the techniques together for the same dish. It can seem intimidating when you're looking at the dish, which is why we're going to go over the basics right now and set you up for future delicious dishes.

Steaming (Dum)

Dum is the name of the technique of cooking a dish in its own steams. In cooking with a slow cooker, you will often be using a variation of this technique. This is accomplished in a slow cooker by putting the lid on top of the slow cooker and allowing none of the steam to really escape.

Dum allows the dish to keep the smell and flavors sealed inside. In the past, they would use wheat flour dough to seal the container and then set the pot on hot coals. There, the dish would cook until it was completed. Obviously, you won't be using the wheat flour dough with our recipes, but it is really interesting to know how the style of cooking was originally done.

Tempering (Baghar or Tadka)

When you use tempering, you're going to seasoning your dish with a hot oil that has spices already in it. This kind of seasoning can happen at the beginning of a recipe or towards the end. It will depend entirely on the dish.

In order to infuse the oil, you will heat the oil until it begins almost smoking. At that point, you'll turn the heat way down, then add the spices. After this, you put the oil in the dish.

There is a little bit of danger that you will need to keep in mind when you are doing this dish. When you add the ingredients to the oil, it is likely that oil will bubble and fly around you. You will need to move quickly and make sure that you are protected from the oil that might splash on you. You'll also want to avoid adding water to this mixture as it will cause the oil to splash and will reduce the flavors of the dish.

Add the ingredients to the oil one at a time to make sure that you're getting the most out of each ingredient. You should work from whole spices to the herbs to the powders.

Sautéing (Bhunao)

This is one of the most common ways of cooking foods in all of Indian cooking. You will saute the ingredients over medium to high heat. You'll have to constantly stir the ingredients while you are going. When you are doing this, you might want to add some water to the ingredients. This will keep them from sticking to the pan while you are cooking them.

This sautéing technique will bring out the best flavors of the ingredients. But you might be uncertain about how long you need to saute things, but you should saute the ingredients until the fat separates from the mixture that you are cooking.

Grilling (Tandoori Cooking)

In the past, cooking in the kitchen has been done in clay ovens which are also known as tandoors. The recipes in this book don't require you to have a tandoor. They have been adjusted to better fit with the grill or oven in your kitchen.

Tandoori cooking can also include some marinating. We have included times in our recipes to make sure that you're getting the most out of the flavors in your dish. You'll definitely want to keep the dishes marinating for as long as possible.

Deep-Frying (Talina)

Deep frying is another well-known way of making dishes in India. Typically people will use a wok or something similar in shape and depth for the oil. In this case, you might feel more comfortable using a deep fryer. There are differing opinions about how you should treat the oil for your deep frying. Common knowledge is using new oil every time. But some people like to reuse the oil. You'll want to let the oil heat up between batches of frying things. This will make sure that everything goes according to plan. You should be using just enough oil for the things that you are trying to fry. Using too much can actually be hard.

Essential Ingredients

When it comes to Indian cooking, there are some common ingredients that you will need to be aware of. They are necessary for every dish and they might be a little bit odd for you. But once you've figured out these different flavors, you'll really be able to make each dish unique and interesting.

Spices and Spice Mixes

There are many spices that are used in Indian dishes. They are found in many forms which means that there are tons of ways to really put them together. With mixes, you'll want to create mixes of spices when you need them. You don't want to have them prepared in advance because you want to make sure that all of the spices are the best they can be. However, if you don't have the time to create the mixes, you'll be able to find premade mixes in Indian grocery stores. You'll have to be very careful with the dates on the package as you want to make sure that you are getting good spices and not old ones.

Ginger-Garlic Paste

This mixture, in particular, is very important in this recipe book. In order to help you get the most out of it, we have included a recipe here so you don't have to search for one on your own. You may also be able to find a paste already mixed in an Indian grocery store. This mixture is a little bit tricky since it can cook quickly and possibly burn. You'll want to have your eyes on it while you are cooking.

Oil

When cooking Indian dishes, you will find that ghee (clarified butter) is one of the most common cooking mediums. However, you may want to use light vegetable oil instead. Ghee can provide a unique flavor to the dishes that you are making. In other areas of India, they also use mustard oil. This particular oil is more pungent and has to be heated up to its smoking point before you use it in the cooking process.

You will not find olive oil used in traditional Indian dishes. Olive oil can cause spices to lose their flavors. As well, olive oil burns more easily and cannot often stand up to the high heat required for Indian dishes.

Souring Agents

Indian dishes require so many different flavors all in one dish. In order to get the sour flavors into a dish, you will need special things to bring in the flavor. You will find that tamarind, lime or lemon juice, tomatoes, vinegar, and sometimes yogurt can be used to make a dish have a slightly sour flavor.

Tamarind and lemon juice can replace one another. If you need a souring agent that isn't wet, you will probably use amchoor or dried mango powder in order to get that flavor.

Tenderizer

In order to tenderize meat, you will often use papaya and yogurt. In this book, we also suggest pineapple as a tenderizer instead of just those two.

Thickening Agent

In order to get the body that you need from the sauces in some dishes, you will find that yogurt, chickpea flour, nut pastes, and onions are used. They can really make a sauce thicker and more appealing.

How to Cook with Spices

Spices are a definitely important part of Indian cooking. There is a lot to know about these spices. Ancient texts will often talk about how they can help the human body, preserve dishes, and add flavor to food. The ancient Indian art of healing, known as Ayurveda, focuses in particular on how food plays into the health and well-being of individuals. The texts say that in a single meal or at least once a day, you should have sweet, salty, tangy, and hot flavors. Flavors like these can be provided by spices.

Spice Combinations

When it comes to using spices, they can provide a complex flavor to seemingly simple dishes. But you also have to know how they work together. While there is no right way to mix spices, playing with spices will allow you to find the mixes that you like the most. If you're new, then you might want to take advantage of the fact that there are premade spice mixtures in Indian grocery stores everywhere. These can also just save you some time.

But when it comes to Indian food, you will want to really pay attention to the spices. There is a learning curve of understanding the flavors when they should be added to dishes, and the order you should add them is incredibly important.

Some of the spices need to be cooked to get the most out of their flavors. There are some spices like cloves and raw green cardamom that can be used raw and as a garnish.

How to Prepare Spices

When you are preparing your spices, you need to make sure that you're doing everything right. There are several different ways to prepare spices, so we'll make sure that you're doing everything the right way.

When using oil or ghee for cooking the spices, you will need to make sure that you're getting the oil hot before you're adding the spices. Hot oil is going to retain the flavors of the spices that you are using. If the oil is cold, then you will not get as much flavor. Ghee can be heated quite hot and it will hold the flavors of spices a little bit better than most oils.

When roasting spices, you'll want to make sure that your skillet is dry. You will also want to make sure that you've gotten the skillet hot before you start adding the spices. You'll have to be prepared to move quickly as some of the spices will heat up quickly and can burn.

Also, make sure that you're making the proper substitutions of ingredients when you're trying to substitute things. Some ingredients like coriander powder cannot be replaced by fresh coriander. If you are uncertain about what can be replaced with what, use the index and we'll help you find the right substitution. You will also find that replacing ground spices instead of whole spices is something that you can easily do. The strength of the flavor goes down when you're using the powder, but that can be good sometimes.

You will want to taste your dishes often to adjust the seasonings that you are adding. You will want to make sure that your dish isn't getting overspiced. When you are starting out, you will struggle a little bit to understand exactly how everything works together. As you learn how the spices work, you will be able to change how you use them in each dish with ease.

Before you start cooking, you'll want to make sure that your spices are ready. Many of these recipes will require your spices to be ready to go one right after the other. So make sure that you have them set up and ready to go for when you need them.

Finally, if you burn your spices, just toss them out. You will not want to add the burned ones because they aren't going to taste good.

Basic Spices

These are the spices that you are going to need if you are cooking a lot of Indian food.

Red chili (powder and whole)

Salt

Coriander (powder and whole)

Cumin seeds

Turmeric

Bay Leaves

Mustard Seeds

Cinnamon

Black peppercorns

Cloves

Black and green cardamom

Mango powder

Carom seeds (also known as ajwain or ajowan)

Dried fenugreek leaves

Tamarind pulp

How to Grind and Store Spices

When using spices, the first thing is making sure that you are using the freshest possible ingredients. You will probably want to replace your spices once a year if you aren't using them all the time. In order to test the freshness of your ingredients, you can smell them. If the spices aren't that smelly, then the spice has probably lost the potency that it once had. This is true for spices that are on their own and it is also true for spices that are mixed.

When you are grinding spices, you can use a mortar and pestle. You can also use a coffee grinder, although you will want to have a coffee grinder that is only for the spices that you are preparing.

When storing spices, you will want to keep them in a cupboard or drawer that is far away from direct sunlight. You will also want to keep things in a glass or plastic containers. This will allow you to see how much of the spice that you have.

You will want to avoid using damp utensils when getting spices from the jar. Keeping moisture away will make sure that the ingredients are lasting as long as possible. Storing ingredients in the fridge can keep them fresher especially if you live in a particularly hot area.

Tools

When it comes to cooking, there a variety of tools that you will need. We will, of course, need a slow cooker for all of the recipes in this book, but there are many more tools that you will need.

A deep pan (preferably nonstick)

Blender

Tempering pan also know as Tadke ka bartan (1- to 2-cup capacity specifically for tempering)

Sieve

Spice grinder (mortar and pestle, coffee grinder, etc.)

Food processor

These tools are going to be the specialty tools that you need. There are other tools that you will need, but most of them will already be in your kitchen.

Masaledani

In every Indian kitchen, there is a masaledani. It is a spice box that contains 5 or 6 of the most basic spices. You'll need these spices a lot when you are cooking. In order to help make them less intimidating, we will be going over the basics of these spices.

Turmeric (Haldi)

This is one spice that you have to have. Regardless of the area of origin, turmeric is going to make an appearance in almost all of the dishes from India. You will find that this spice is very similar to ginger, so it may even look like gingerroot when you are picking it up. Fresh turmeric has a particularly strong flavor, but it is often used in a more mild, ground form. In addition to flavor, turmeric adds color to food. It is even considered the Indian equivalent of saffron.

The yellow color and mild flavor are great, but turmeric can also be used as a preservative. When you're making pickles, you might use salt and turmeric as a way of keeping them good for years after you've dried them in the sun.

This spice is used to color everything from cheese to spice mixes, yogurt to salad dressing. It can also help by reducing inflammation and being used as an antiseptic. When you have a cut or bruise, you may want to rub a paste made from turmeric on it. This mixture will help you. Turmeric and warm milk can be combined to help reduce a fever as well.

Thanks to all of the properties of turmeric, there is a special place in the kitchens and homes of Indians for this spice. It is especially important for Hindu households.

Chili Powder (Lal Mirch)

Chili probably made its way into India when Vasco da Gama, a Portuguese explorer, came to the country. The spice has made its way into many of the dishes. The climate of India actually worked well with chilis and many varieties are grown across the country. Chili powder in Indian is very similar to cayenne pepper. However, unlike other areas, the ground pepper is going to be purely the ground pepper. In other parts of the world, ground pepper is sometimes combined with salt and other spices.

These peppers are going to anywhere from orange to dark red and have quite a bit to them. If you aren't able to stomach the spices, then you might need Kashmiri lal mirch. It is the milder version of chili powder and will have some color that it can add to dishes. Some people will use Kashmiri lal mirch purely for the color that it can give to a dish. Chili powder is useful in almost all dishes as many Indian dishes tend to be on the spicy side.

Cumin (Jeera)

Cumin is another of the common spices. There are several ways that cumin is found. You can find it whole or ground. It also comes in two different forms: black and white. Black cumin, also called royal cumin, is a little bit sweeter. It is also a little bit harder to find than white cumin.

However, cumin, in general, has a warm and earthy flavor. This makes it great for soups and stews. You'll find that when you roast cumin, you will have a good flavor to add to cheese and bread. If you have roasted and ground cumin, then you'll want to add it to raita which is a yogurt-based dip. Cumin can help with your digestion, so you'll find it in the Indian form of lemonade, jal jeera.

Asafetida (Heeng)

Asafetida is a bit strong and can smell a little bit like sulfur. This can make it hard to imagine using, but the odor is something that you will smell all over the entire plant when you are cooking. This spice isn't often found in the west, but Indians use it in many different dishes.

It has a delicious flavor when added to dishes in oil. But you'll find that it has great medicinal properties. It can help with digestive issues. It can also help with lung-related issues and diseases like bronchitis and asthma. When people were a little more superstitious, they would use this spice to keep the evil spirits away from children. There are even some beliefs that it can help with anxiety and alcoholism.

This spice is mainly used for lentil dishes. You only need a pinch and sometimes even less in oil to season a whole dish. This is quite a potent spice.

Mustard Seeds (Sarson)

Mustard is a spice that people know all around the world, but it is very common in India. People will use cooked mustard greens to powdered mustard seeds. The flavors are very common. In the western parts of the world, you'll find that most people use yellow mustard, but black mustard is much more common in India.

Mustard seeds are part of salad dressing, vegetable dishes, and curry. The oil that you can get from mustard seeds is as common as olive oil is in Italy. Mustard oil was used long before vegetable oil made its way into the market, but it isn't just used for cooking. It is also used for body massages as well. The health benefits that you get from the oil are very helpful. It is a long strong tasting, so that might take some time to get used to.

Coriander Seeds (Dhaniya)

This is the last ingredient on our list, but it isn't something that you should forget. The smells of this spice are going to make your kitchen smell amazing. Coriander is known in the US as cilantro, but it is also very common in India. It is used in many sauces and as a garnish.

The fruits of this plant have seeds that have a sweet, citrus flavor and a nutty smell to them. This is a staple in the Indian kitchen. You will be able to buy whole seeds and roast them on your own. After roasting, you will want to crush them to use in other ways. You can also make a powder and use it in curries and things. There are many different ways to use these seeds, but they will always be at home in Indian cuisine.

Making Recipes Slow Cooker Friendly

When it comes to making a recipe work in a slow cooker, many will translate easily. You'll be cooking ingredients in a little bit of liquid for a long period of time. You'll be able to play with these recipes and make them work a slow cooker even when they weren't meant to.

But you'll find that some recipes will be a little bit more difficult. Deep frying food in a slow cooker isn't going to work as well, but braising or stewing recipes are going to work easily.

You will even be able to prepare dried beans in the slow cooker. It will involve a little bit of work since you will have to soak them overnight, but it can work really well and cost you just a little bit less than canned beans. But canned beans can save you a little bit of time in the long run.

Improvisation and Shortcuts

Don't be afraid to put your own spin on things according to your unique tastes and preferences. Every recipe looks a little different in different households, so make sure that you try to take the time to make the recipe your own.

Meat

When cooking meat in a slow cooker, you will not have your meat browned in the cooker. If you want browned meat, then you're going to need to brown it a little bit before you add it to the slow cooker. Just searing the meat or quickly sautéing it will allow it to look brown.

If you are making a stew and need a thick broth, then you can coat the meat in flour. This will not only speed up the sautéing and browning but also help thicken the sauce.

Slow cooking works well with the cheaper, leaner cuts of meat that you need to cook for longer before they become tender. If you are transposing a recipe from oven or stovetop, then you might need to pick a leaner cut of meat that will be better suited to being in the slow cooker.

Make sure that you're not overcooking thing. Poultry tends to cook quickly, so just four hours on low will be enough. Poultry will turn out better when you are using wet ingredients in the slow cooker as well as it will make sure that the lean meat will not dry out.

When you're using a slow cooker, you will save time by not having to marinate your food. The marinating process happens in the slow cooker as it takes hours and hours for the flavors to become part of the dish.

LENTIL RECIPES

Spiced Coconut Lentils

Total Time: 8 hours 20 minutes

Serves: 12

3 cups yellow lentils, Soak for 10 minutes
14 oz coconut milk
1/4 cup cilantro
1 tbsp fresh ginger, peeled and chopped
2 tbsp curry powder
2 tsp ground cumin
2 tsp ground turmeric
1 tsp chili powder
4 chilies, stemmed and seeded
1 large onion, chopped
5 garlic cloves
1/2 tsp sugar
28 oz can tomatoes, diced
Kosher salt

- Rinse lentil and drain well. Add lentil into the slow cooker.
- Add sugar, chili powder, turmeric, cumin, curry powder, ginger, garlic, onion, and Serrano chilies into the food processor and process until mixture becomes a paste. Add into the slow cooker.
- Stir in tomatoes and 6 cups of water.
- Cover slow cooker and cook on low for 8 hours.
- Season with salt and stir well.
- Add coconut milk and stir well.
- Garnish with cilantro and serve.

Calories 258, Fat 8 g, Carbohydrates 33 g, Sugar 4 g, Protein 13 g, Cholesterol 0 mg

Healthy Lentil Curry

Total Time: 5 hours 10 minutes

Serves: 6

1 1/2 cups green lentils, rinse and drained
3 tbsp tomato paste
14 oz can coconut milk
3 tsp curry powder
1 onion, diced
3 garlic cloves, minced
1 yellow pepper, diced
1/4 tsp pepper

1/2 tsp ground ginger
2 tsp garam masala
2 tsp sugar
2 1/2 cups water
2 tbsp olive oil
1 tsp garlic powder
1 tsp cumin
1 1/2 tsp salt

- Add olive oil, yellow pepper, garlic, and onion into the slow cooker.
- Add lentils into the slow cooker and stir well.
- Add all remaining ingredients and stir well.
- Cover and cook on low for 5 hours.
- Stir well and serve with rice.

Calories 376, Fat 19 g, Carbohydrates 39 g, Sugar 4 g, Protein 15 g, Cholesterol 0 mg

Delicious Black Lentil Curry

Total Time: 12 hours 15 minutes

Serves: 8

1 cup whole black gram lentils	1 cinnamon stick
3 cloves	3 cardamom pods
1 tbsp ginger, chopped	1/2 tsp chili powder
8 garlic cloves, chopped	4 tomatoes, diced
2 green chilies, cut lengthwise	1 tsp garam masala
1 tbsp coriander powder	1/4 cup cream
1/2 tsp turmeric powder	2 tbsp butter
1/2 cup kidney beans	Salt
1 bay leaf	

- Soak black lentils and kidney beans in water for overnight.
- Add all ingredients except cream into the slow cooker with 4 cups water and stir well.
- Cover and cook on low for 12 hours.
- Stir well and lightly mash using the back of a spoon.
- Add cream and stir well.
- Serve and enjoy.

Calories 186, Fat 4 g, Carbohydrates 27 g, Sugar 2 g, Protein 10 g, Cholesterol 9 mg

Lentil Butternut Squash Curry

Total Time: 12 hours 15 minutes

Serves: 8

2 cups red lentils
4 cups butternut squash, cut into cubes
2 tbsp ginger, minced
1 1/2 tsp curry powder
1 tsp ground coriander
1 onion, minced
2 garlic cloves, minced

1 tsp garam masala
1 tsp turmeric
14 oz can coconut milk
19 oz can tomatoes, diced
3 cups vegetable stock
1 tsp ground cumin
1/2 tsp salt

- Add all ingredients into the slow cooker and stir well.
- Cover and cook on low for 8 hours.
- Serve and enjoy.

Calories 329, Fat 11 g, Carbohydrates 45 g, Sugar 5 g, Protein 15 g, Cholesterol 0 mg

Simple Slow Cooker Lentil

Total Time: 6 hours 15 minutes

Serves: 6

2 cups red lentils, rinsed and drained
1 bay leaf
1 tbsp ground turmeric
1 tbsp fresh ginger, grated
1 medium onion, diced
15 oz can tomatoes, diced

5 cups water
1 tsp fennel seeds
2 tsp mustard seeds
2 tsp cumin seeds
1/4 tsp ground black pepper
1 tsp kosher salt

- Heat pan over medium heat and toast fennel seeds, mustard seeds, and cumin seeds in a pan until fragrant for 2-3 minutes.
- Add toasted spices and remaining all ingredients into the slow cooker and stir well.
- Cover and cook on low for 6 hours.
- Stir well and serve.

Calories 265, Fat 1 g, Carbohydrates 46 g, Sugar 4 g, Protein 18 g, Cholesterol 0 mg

Lentil Potato Coconut Curry

Total Time: 8 hours 15 minutes

Serves: 10

2 cups brown lentils

14 oz can coconut milk

3 cups vegetable broth

15 oz can tomato sauce

15 oz can tomatoes, diced

1/4 tsp ground cloves

3 tbsp curry powder

2 medium carrots, peel and diced

1 sweet potato, peel and diced

2 garlic cloves, minced

1 medium onion, diced

- Add all ingredients except coconut milk into the slow cooker and stir well.
- Cover and cook on low for 8 hours.
- Stir in coconut milk and serve with rice.

Calories 152, Fat 3 g, Carbohydrates 22 g, Sugar 6 g, Protein 9 g, Cholesterol 0 mg

Spicy Lentil Stew

Total Time: 6 hours 15 minutes

Serves: 8

3 cups red lentils, rinsed and drained

3 1/2 cup tomatoes, crushed

1/2 tbsp black pepper

1/2 tbsp curry powder

1/2 tbsp paprika

1/2 tbsp chili powder

1/2 tbsp garam masala

1/2 tbsp turmeric powder

6 cups vegetable broth

1 onion, diced

2 garlic cloves, minced

3 Serrano chili, diced

2 tbsp cilantro, minced

1 tbsp Creole seasoning

1 tbsp garlic powder

1 tbsp onion powder

1/2 tbsp ginger powder

- Add all ingredients into the slow cooker and stir well.
- Cover and cook on high for 5 hours.
- Uncover the slow cooker and cook for another 50 minutes.
- Serve and enjoy.

Calories 318, Fat 2 g, Carbohydrates 51 g, Sugar 5 g, Protein 23 g, Cholesterol 0 mg

Gluten Free Masala Lentils

Total Time: 6 hours 10 minutes

Serves: 8

2 1/4 cups brown lentils
4 cups vegetable broth
15 oz can tomatoes, diced
1 medium onion, chopped
3 garlic cloves, minced
1 tbsp fresh ginger, minced

1/4 cup tomato paste
2 tsp tamarind paste
1 tsp maple syrup
1 1/2 tsp garam masala
1 cup coconut milk
3/4 tsp salt

- Add all ingredients except coconut milk into the slow cooker and stir well.
- Cover and cook on low for 6 hours.
- Stir in coconut milk and serve.

Calories 306, Fat 9 g, Carbohydrates 41 g, Sugar 5 g, Protein 17 g, Cholesterol 0 mg

Flavorful Red Lentils Curry

Total Time: 8 hours 15 minutes

Serves: 16

4 cups brown lentils, rinsed and drained
5 tbsp red curry paste
1 tbsp garam masala
1 1/2 tsp turmeric
2 tsp sugar
1/2 cup coconut milk

29 oz can tomato puree
2 onions, diced
4 garlic cloves, minced
1 tbsp ginger, minced
4 tbsp butter
7 cups water
1 tsp salt

- Add all ingredients except coconut milk into the slow cooker and stir well.
- Cover and cook on low for 8 hours.
- Add coconut milk and stir well.
- Serve with rice and enjoy.

Calories 261, Fat 6 g, Carbohydrates 37 g, Sugar 4 g, Protein 13 g, Cholesterol 8 mg

Cauliflower Lentil Curry

Total Time: 5 hours 15 minutes

Serves: 6

1 cup red lentils

3 cups cauliflower, cut into florets

3 dates, pitted and chopped

2/3 cup coconut milk

1 1/2 tsp turmeric

1 tsp ginger, grated

2 tbsp Thai red curry paste

3 garlic cloves, minced

1/2 onion, chopped

3 cups vegetable broth

1/4 tsp sea salt

- Add all ingredients except coconut milk into the slow cooker and stir well.
- Cover and cook on low for 5 hours.
- Add coconut milk and stir well.
- Serve with rice and enjoy.

Calories 247, Fat 9 g, Carbohydrates 29 g, Sugar 6 g, Protein 12 g, Cholesterol 0 mg

Delicious Tempered Lentils

Total Time: 6 hours 20 minutes

Serves: 6

1 1/2 cups yellow split lentils, rinsed and drained
1/4 cup fresh cilantro, chopped
1 tsp turmeric powder
2 tsp garlic, minced
2 medium tomatoes, chopped
1/2 medium onion, chopped
1 tsp salt

For tempering:
2 tbsp vegetable oil
1/4 tsp chili powder
1/2 tsp coriander powder
1/2 tsp cumin powder
1 garlic cloves, minced
1/2 tsp whole cumin seeds

- Add lentils into the slow cooker with 4 cups water.
- Add turmeric powder, garlic, tomatoes, onion, and salt into the slow cooker and stir well.
- Cover and cook on low for 5 hours.
- Heat vegetable oil in the pan over medium-high heat.
- Once the oil is hot then turn off the heat and add cumin, garlic, and spices. Mix well.
- Stir prepared tempering into the hot lentil.
- Add cilantro and stir well.
- Cook lentils for another 1 hour to blend all flavors.
- Serve hot with rice and enjoy.

Calories 208, Fat 5.2 g, Carbohydrates 28 g, Sugar 1.5 g, Protein 12.7 g, Cholesterol 0 mg

Lentil Sweet Potato Soup

Total Time: 6 hours 20 minutes

Serves: 4

1 1/2 cups brown lentils
1 large sweet potato, cut into 1/2 inch cubes
6 cups vegetable broth
1 cup coconut milk
1/2 tbsp chili paste
1 medium onion, diced
3 garlic cloves, minced

1/2 tbsp ginger, grated
2 tsp ground cumin
1 tsp garam masala
2 tsp lime juice
1/4 cup fresh cilantro, chopped
14 oz can tomatoes, diced
Pepper
Salt

- Add all ingredients except tomatoes and lime juice into the slow cooker and stir well.
- Cover and cook on low for 6 hours.
- Stir in tomatoes and lime juice.
- Cook soup for another 10 minutes to blend the flavors.
- Season with pepper and salt.
- Serve warm and enjoy.

Calories 395, Fat 17 g, Carbohydrates 54 g, Sugar 11 g, Protein 23 g, Cholesterol 1 mg

Potato Red Lentil Curry

Total Time: 4 hours 15 minutes

Serves: 8

1 cup red lentils, rinsed	14 oz can tomato, diced
2 potatoes, cut into cubed	14 oz can coconut milk
1 cup brown lentil, rinsed	1 tbsp garlic, minced
1 large onion, diced	1 tsp ginger, minced
1/2 tsp turmeric	2 tbsp butter
1/2 tsp cumin seeds, toasted	2 tbsp curry powder
1 tsp sugar	1/2 tsp red pepper flakes

- Add all ingredients except coconut milk into the slow cooker and stir well.
- Add water into the slow cooker to cover lentil mixture.
- Cover and cook on high for 4 hours.
- Add coconut milk and stir well.
- Serve warm and enjoy.

Calories 307, Fat 14 g, Carbohydrates 39 g, Sugar 3 g, Protein 13 g, Cholesterol 8 mg

Healthy Spinach Lentils

Total Time: 4 hours 30 minutes

Serves: 4

1 cup yellow split peas
3 1/2 cups water
10 oz spinach, chopped
1 tsp cumin seeds
1 tbsp fresh ginger, peeled and minced
3 garlic cloves, minced
1 tsp mustard seeds

1 medium onion, diced
15 oz can tomatoes, drained and diced
2 jalapeno pepper, cored and diced
1 tsp turmeric
1/2 tsp coriander
1/4 tsp cayenne
1 tsp salt

- Add all ingredients except spinach into the slow cooker and stir well.
- Cover and cook on high for 4 hours.
- Add spinach and cook for another 20.
- Stir well and serve.

Calories 236, Fat 1.4 g, Carbohydrates 43 g, Sugar 9 g, Protein 16.1 g, Cholesterol 0 mg

Easy Lentils Rice

Total Time: 4 hours 10 minutes

Serves: 6

1/2 cup lentils, rinsed and drained
1 tsp garlic powder
3 1/2 cups vegetable broth
1 tbsp curry powder

1 cup white rice, rinsed and drained
1 onion, diced
1/4 tsp pepper
Salt

- Add all ingredients into the slow cooker and stir well.
- Cover and cook on high for 4 hours.
- Stir well and serve.

Calories 204, Fat 1.3 g, Carbohydrates 37 g, Sugar 1.7 g, Protein 9.6 g, Cholesterol 0 mg

Lentil Chicken Vegetable Curry

Total Time: 4 hours 20 minutes

Serves: 8

1 lb dried lentils, rinsed and drained
4 cups fresh spinach, chopped
4 cups vegetable broth
1/4 tsp cinnamon
1 1/2 tsp turmeric
1/2 tsp cayenne
1 tbsp curry powder

2 lbs chicken thighs, boneless and cut into pieces
6 garlic cloves, minced
1 small cauliflower head, cut into florets
2 cups carrots, chopped
1 large onion, chopped
1 tsp salt

- Add all ingredients except spinach into the slow cooker and stir well.
- Cover and cook on high for 3 1/2 hours.
- Add spinach and stir well. Cover and cook for another 30 minutes.
- Stir well and serve with rice.

Calories 473, Fat 10 g, Carbohydrates 42 g, Sugar 4.6 g, Protein 51 g, Cholesterol 101 mg

Healthy Green Lentil Curry

Total Time: 6 hours 15 minutes

Serves: 6

2 cups green lentils, rinsed and drained

3 cups water

6 oz can tomato paste

14 oz can coconut milk

1 tsp cumin

1 tsp curry powder

1/2 tsp ground coriander

1 tsp turmeric

1 tsp vegetable oil

6 garlic cloves, minced

1 large onion, chopped

1 1/4 tsp salt

- Heat oil in the pan over medium heat.
- Add garlic and onion to the pan and sauté for 5 minutes.
- Add cumin, curry powder, coriander, turmeric, and salt and sauté for 1 minute.
- Transfer pan mixture to the slow cooker with remaining all ingredients. Stir well.
- Cover and cook on low for 6 hours.
- Serve warm with rice and enjoy.

Calories 404, Fat 15.9 g, Carbohydrates 49 g, Sugar 5.9 g, Protein 19.7 g, Cholesterol 0 mg

Smokey Lentil Soup

Total Time: 6 hours 15 minutes

Serves: 6

2 cups red lentils
2 tbsp smoked paprika
2 carrots, chopped
4 garlic cloves, minced
8 cups vegetable broth
1 onion, chopped

3 tbsp fresh parsley, chopped
1/4 cup hulled pumpkin seeds
2 potatoes, peeled and chopped
1/3 cup tomato paste
3 tbsp lemon juice
3 tbsp vegetable oil

- Add lentils, lemon juice, tomato paste, garlic, paprika, carrots, potato, onion, and broth into the slow cooker and stir well.
- Cover and cook on low for 6 hours.
- Meanwhile, in a small bowl, combine together parsley and oil.
- Ladle soup into the bowls and drizzle with parsley and oil mixture.
- Sprinkle pumpkin seeds over the soup.
- Serve and enjoy.

Calories 474, Fat 9.9 g, Carbohydrates 67.6 g, Sugar 7 g, Protein 25.8 g, Cholesterol 0 mg

Spinach Coconut Lentil Soup

Total Time: 4 hours 45 minutes

Serves: 6

4 cups fresh spinach, chopped
14 oz coconut milk
4 cups vegetable stock
1 1/2 cup red lentils, rinsed and drained
1 tsp ground cinnamon
1/2 tsp garam masala
1 tsp ground turmeric

1 tsp ground coriander seed
1 tsp ground cumin
2 tsp garlic, minced
1 large onion, chopped
1 tbsp vegetable oil
Pepper
Salt

- Heat oil in the pan over medium heat.
- Add onion to the pan and sauté for 5 minutes or until golden brown.
- Add cinnamon, garam masala, turmeric, coriander, cumin, and garlic and cook for 2 minutes.
- Transfer onion-spice mixture into the slow cooker.
- Add lentils and stock into the slow cooker and stir well.
- Cover and cook on low for 4 hours.
- Add coconut milk and spinach. Stir well and cook for another 30 minutes.
- Season with pepper and salt.
- Serve and enjoy.

Calories 368, Fat 20 g, Carbohydrates 37 g, Sugar 5 g, Protein 14.9 g, Cholesterol 0 mg

Spicy Keema Lentils

Total Time: 4 hours 15 minutes

Serves: 4

3 cups green lentils, cooked

1 tsp dried chili flakes

1/2 tsp ground turmeric

2 tsp garam masala

2 tsp ground coriander

2 tsp ground cumin

1 large onion, chopped

3 tbsp fresh ginger, grated

6 garlic cloves, chopped

1 1/2 cup vegetable broth

2 tbsp tamari

1 tsp pepper

1 tsp salt

- Add all ingredients into the slow cooker and stir well.
- Cover and cook on low for 4 hours.
- Stir well and serve.

Calories 206, Fat 0.9 g, Carbohydrates 37 g, Sugar 2 g Protein 15 g, Cholesterol 0 mg

Creamy Split Pea Curry

Total Time: 6 hours 15 minutes

Serves: 6

1 1/2 cups dried split peas
1 cup heavy cream
1/2 tsp ground ginger
2 tsp curry powder
1 tbsp turmeric
1 tbsp green curry paste

3 garlic cloves, minced
1/2 cup onion, diced
15 oz can coconut milk
28 oz can tomatoes, crushed
1 tsp salt

- Add all ingredients except cream into the slow cooker. Stir well.
- Cover and cook on low for 6 hours.
- Add cream and stir well.
- Serve with rice and enjoy.

Calories 425, Fat 23.8 g, Carbohydrates 42.4 g, Sugar 9 g, Protein 15.5 g, Cholesterol 27 mg

Lentil Vegetable Soup

Total Time: 8 hours 15 minutes

Serves: 8

1 1/2 cups green lentils, rinsed and drained
9 cups vegetable broth
5 peppercorns
3 bay leaves
3 tbsp soy sauce
1 tsp thyme

2 tsp oregano
1 tbsp garlic powder
2 cups corn
4 cups potatoes, diced
3 large carrots, diced
3 large celery stalks, diced
2 medium onion, diced

- Add all ingredients into the slow cooker and mix well.
- Cover and cook on low for 8 hours.
- Discard peppercorns and bay leaves from soup and using blender puree the soup until you get desired texture.
- Serve hot and enjoy.

Calories 288, Fat 2.6 g, Carbohydrates 49 g, Sugar 6.7 g, Protein 18.5 g, Cholesterol 0 mg

Delicious Lemon Lentils

Total Time: 2 hours 45 minutes

Serves: 8

1 1/2 cups pink lentils

1 tbsp milk

2 tbsp lemon juice

2 Serrano chilies, sliced

1 tbsp fresh ginger, minced

4 garlic cloves, sliced

1 small onion, diced

5 cups water

1 1/2 tsp salt

- Add all ingredients except milk and lemon juice into the slow cooker. Stir well.
- Cover and cook on high for 2 1/2 hours.
- Add lemon juice and stir well.
- Add milk and stir well and serve.

Calories 135, Fat 0.9 g, Carbohydrates 23.4 g, Sugar 0.6 g, Protein 9.4 g, Cholesterol 0 mg

Tasty Carrot Lentils Soup

Total Time: 8 hours 15 minutes

Serves: 8

1/2 cup lentils
2 lbs carrots, peeled and cut into 1-inch pieces
1/2 tsp harissa
1/4 cup maple syrup
1 cup orange juice
4 cups vegetable broth

1 tsp fresh ginger, grated
1/2 tbsp ground cumin
1/2 tbsp curry powder
1 medium onion, peeled and chopped
Pepper
Salt

- Add orange juice, broth, ginger, curry powder, onion, and carrots into the slow cooker and mix well.
- Cover and cook on low for 6 hours.
- Add lentils, harissa, and maple syrup. Stir well and cook on high for another 2 hours.
- Season with pepper and salt.
- Serve and enjoy.

Calories 158, Fat 1.1 g, Carbohydrates 30.6 g Sugar 15.3 g Protein 7 g, Cholesterol 0 mg

Lentil Sweet Potato Beans Stew

Total Time: 6 hours 30 minutes

Serves: 6

3/4 cup dry lentils, rinsed and drained
3 cups sweet potatoes, cut into 1 inch cubed
1 1/2 cups green beans, cut into pieces
1 1/2 cups baby carrots
1/2 cup plain yogurt
1 3/4 cup vegetable broth

2 garlic cloves, minced
1 tsp fresh ginger, chopped
1 tsp ground cumin
1 tbsp curry powder
2 tbsp vegetable oil
1/4 cup onion, chopped
1/4 tsp black pepper
1/2 tsp salt

- Add lentils, carrots, onion, and sweet potatoes into the slow cooker.
- In a pan, heat oil over medium heat.
- Add garlic, ginger, pepper, cumin, curry powder, and salt and stir for 1 minute. Stir in broth.
- Pour mixture into the slow cooker and mix well.
- Cover and cook on low for 6 hours.
- Turn heat to high and stir in green beans. Cover and cook for another 15 minutes.
- Top with plain yogurt and serve.

Calories 269, Fat 5.9 g, Carbohydrates 43.5 g, Sugar 4.8 g, Protein 10.8 g, Cholesterol 1 mg

BEANS AND PEAS RECIPES

Healthy Chickpeas and Tofu 45
Chickpea Pumpkin Lentil Curry 46
North Indian red Beans 47
Simple Black Eyed Peas 48
Tasty Black Eyed Pea Curry 49
Healthy Green Pea and Cauliflower Korma 50
Red Beans Bowl 51
Chickpea Lentil Chili 52
Red Beans and Lentils 53
Simple Chickpea Curry 54
Pea Chickpea Vegetable Curry 55
Perfect Curried Baked Beans 56

Red Beans with Bell Pepper 57
Spicy Black Eyed Peas 58
Chickpea Coconut Quinoa Curry 59
Red Beans Cabbage Soup 60
Gluten Free Chickpea Curry 61
Vegetarian Chili Bowl 62
Healthy Turmeric Lentil Bean Chili 63
Chickpea Kale Sweet Potato Stew 64
Chickpea Spinach Cauliflower Curry 65
Spicy Winter Chickpeas 66
Spicy Curried Chickpeas 67
Spiced Green Peas Rice 68
Buttered Peas Rice 69

Healthy Chickpeas and Tofu

Total Time: 4 hours 15 minutes

Serves: 6

12 oz firm tofu	1 cup tomato puree
15 oz can chickpeas, rinsed and drained	14 oz can coconut milk
	4 garlic cloves, minced
1/8 cup cilantro, chopped	1 medium onion, diced
1/2 tsp ground ginger	1 tsp vegetable oil
2 tsp chili powder	Pepper
1 tbsp curry powder	Salt
1 tbsp garam masala	

- Rinse tofu well and pat dry with paper towel. Squeeze out all liquid from tofu and cut tofu into the pieces.
- Heat oil in the saucepan over medium heat.
- Add onion to the pan and sauté for 5 minutes.
- Add garlic and cook for 1 minute.
- Whisk in coconut milk, ginger, chili powder, curry powder, garam masala, tomato puree, pepper, and salt. Cook for 5 minutes.
- Add chickpeas and tofu into the slow cooker.
- Pour pan mixture into the slow cooker.
- Cover and cook on low for 4 hours.
- Garnish with cilantro and serve.

Calories 294, Fat 18.5 g, Carbohydrates 26.2 g, Sugar 3.3 g, Protein 10.8 g, Cholesterol 0 mg

Chickpea Pumpkin Lentil Curry

Total Time: 8 hours 40 minutes

Serves: 6

15 oz can chickpeas, rinsed and drained
1 cup pumpkin puree
1 cup lentils, rinsed and drained
15 oz can coconut milk
1/4 tsp ground cayenne pepper

1 tbsp curry powder
2 cups vegetable broth
2 garlic cloves, minced
1 medium onion, diced
1 tsp kosher salt

- Add all ingredients except coconut milk into the slow cooker and stir well.
- Cover and cook on low for 8 hours.
- Add coconut milk and stir well. Cook for another 30 minutes.
- Serve with rice and enjoy.

Calories 376, Fat 17 g, Carbohydrates 43.5 g, Sugar 3.1 g, Protein 15.7 g, Cholesterol 0 mg

North Indian red Beans

Total Time: 4 hours 15 minutes

Serves: 4

2 cups dry red beans, soak for overnight

2 tbsp cilantro, chopped

1 cup tomato sauce

1 cinnamon stick

1/4 tsp turmeric

1/4 tsp cayenne pepper

1/4 tsp ground coriander

1 tbsp lemon juice

4 garlic cloves, minced

1 tsp ginger, minced

1 medium onion, chopped

1 tsp cumin seeds

1 bay leaf

1 tbsp vegetable oil

1 1/2 tsp salt

- Heat oil in the pan over medium heat.
- Add onion, bay leaf, and cumin seeds into the pan and cook for 5 minutes.
- Add dry spices and lemon juice and stir for 2 minutes.
- Add beans, cinnamon stick, tomato sauce, and salt into the slow cooker.
- Transfer pan mixture into the slow cooker and stir well.
- Cover and cook on high for 4 hours.
- Using spoon lightly mash the red beans it helps to thicken the gravy.
- Garnish with cilantro and serve.

Calories 376, Fat 4.8 g, Carbohydrates 64.1 g, Sugar 5.9 g, Protein 22.2 g, Cholesterol 0 mg

Simple Black Eyed Peas

Total Time: 6 hours 15 minutes

Serves: 6

1 lb dried black-eyed peas, soak for overnight

1 tsp ground sage

1/8 tsp thyme

1 bay leaf

1 garlic clove, diced

1 small onion, diced

2 cups water

2 cups vegetable broth

1/2 tsp pepper

1 tsp sea salt

- Add all ingredients into the slow cooker and mix well.
- Cover and cook on low for 6 hours.
- Serve and enjoy.

Calories 203,nFat 0.5 g, Carbohydrates 48.8 g, Sugar 2.8 g, Protein 20.2 g, Cholesterol 0 mg

Tasty Black Eyed Pea Curry

Total Time: 4 hours 15 minutes

Serves: 4

1 cup dried black-eyed peas, soaked for overnight

1 bay leaf

6 garlic cloves, minced

1/2 tsp black pepper

1/4 tsp cayenne

2 tomatoes, chopped

3 cups water

1 tsp ginger, minced

1 tsp turmeric

1/2 tsp cumin seeds

1 large onion, diced

1 tsp garam masala

1 tsp salt

- Add all ingredients into the slow cooker and stir well.
- Cover and cook on high for 4 hours.
- Stir well and serve.

Calories 128, Fat 0.4 g, Carbohydrates 31.4 g, Sugar 4.3 g, Protein 10.4 gCholesterol 0 mg

Healthy Green Pea and Cauliflower Korma

Total Time: 4 hours 15 minutes

Serves: 4

10 oz green peas
1 cauliflower head, cut into florets
1 cup water
1 1/2 cups coconut milk
1/4 tsp cayenne

1 tsp turmeric
1/4 tsp cumin
2 tsp garam masala
1 medium onion, diced

- Add all ingredients into the slow cooker and stir well.
- Cover and cook on low for 4 hours.
- Stir well and serve.

Calories 295, Fat 21.9 g, Carbohydrates 21.8 g, Sugar 9.8 g, Protein 7.6 g, Cholesterol 0 mg

Red Beans Bowl

Total Time: 8 hours 15 minutes

Serves: 4

14 oz can kidney beans, drained and rinsed
1/2 tsp garam Masala
1/2 tsp turmeric powder
2 cups onion, chopped
1 tomato, chopped
1/2 inch cinnamon stick
1 bay leaf

2 cloves
1 tsp ginger, minced
5 garlic cloves, minced
1 green chili, chopped
1/2 tbsp cumin seeds
1 tsp cayenne pepper
1 tbsp paprika
Salt

- Add all ingredients except yogurt into the slow cooker and stir well.
- Add 4 cups water and stir to combine.
- Cover and cook on high for 8 hours.
- Using back of spoon mash few beans.
- Stir well and serve with rice.

Calories 399, Fat 2.1 g, Carbohydrates 72.2 g, Sugar 7.4 g, Protein 25.6 g, Cholesterol 2 mg

Chickpea Lentil Chili

Total Time: 8 hours 15 minutes

Serves: 6

1 cup dried chickpeas, soaked overnight
1/2 cup raisins
2 1/2 cups vegetable broth
1/2 cup water
28 oz can whole tomatoes, undrained and crushed
2 cups sweet potatoes, cut into cubes

1 cup lentils
1/2 tsp chili powder
1/2 tsp ground cinnamon
1/4 tsp ground turmeric
1 cup onion, chopped
5 garlic cloves, minced
1 1/2 tsp ground cumin
1 tsp kosher salt

- Add all ingredients into the slow cooker and stir well.
- Cover and cook on low for 8 hours.
- Stir well and serve.

Calories 388, Fat 3.3 g, Carbohydrates 73.3 g, Sugar 17.3 g, Protein 19.6 g, Cholesterol 0 mg

Red Beans and Lentils

Total Time: 4 hours 15 minutes

Serves: 10

3 cups red beans, cooked
1 cup black lentils, rinsed and drained
1/4 tsp ground mustard
1/4 tsp ground nutmeg
1 tsp ground turmeric
1 tsp ground cardamom
1 1/2 tsp chili powder
3 tsp ground cumin

2 tbsp ginger, grated
6 garlic cloves, minced
5 cups water
For serving:
1 tsp garam masala
2 tsp ginger, grated
2 tsp tomato paste
1/2 cup cashew creamer
Salt

- Add all ingredients except serving ingredients into the slow cooker and stir well.
- Cover and cook on high for 4 hours.
- Add all serving ingredients and stir well.
- Serve with rice and enjoy.

Calories 288, Fat 2.8 g, Carbohydrates 49.1 g, Sugar 2 g, Protein 18.4 g, Cholesterol 0 mg

Simple Chickpea Curry

Total Time: 6 hours 10 minutes

Serves: 6

15 oz can chickpeas
15 oz can coconut milk
15 oz can tomatoes, diced
1/4 tbsp cilantro, chopped
2 tbsp curry powder

1 tsp ginger, minced
4 garlic cloves, minced
2 onions, diced
Salt

- Add all ingredients except cilantro into the slow cooker and stir well.
- Cover and cook on low for 6 hours.
- Garnish with cilantro and serve.

Calories 265, Fat 16.3 g, Carbohydrates 27.1 g, Sugar 4.1 g, Protein 6.4 g, Cholesterol 0 mg

Pea Chickpea Vegetable Curry

Total Time: 2 hours 15 minutes

Serves: 8

1 cup can chickpeas, drained	15 oz can coconut milk
1 cup green peas	2 cups vegetable broth
1 tsp red pepper flakes	1 medium onion, diced
1 tsp ground coriander	3/4 cup carrot, diced
1 tsp ginger powder	1 1/2 cups potatoes, chopped
2 tbsp curry powder	2 tsp sea salt

- Add all ingredients into the slow cooker and stir well.
- Cover and cook on high for 2 hours.
- Stir well and serve.

Calories 201, Fat 12.4 g, Carbohydrates 19 g, Sugar 2.7 g, Protein 5.7 g, Cholesterol 0 mg

Perfect Curried Baked Beans

Total Time: 8 hours 10 minutes

Serves: 8

4 cups pinto beans, cooked
1 tbsp vegetable oil
1 medium onion, diced
14 oz can coconut milk
6 oz can tomato paste
2 tbsp brown sugar

1 garlic cloves, minced
1 tbsp fresh ginger, minced
3 tsp curry powder
1/8 tsp red pepper flakes
1/2 tsp cumin
1/2 tsp salt

- Add cooked beans into the slow cooker.
- Heat oil in the pan over medium heat.
- Add onion and sauté for 5 minutes.
- Add garlic and sauté for another 1 minute.
- Stir in crushed red peppers, cumin, curry powder, ginger, and salt.
- Reduce heat and stir in coconut milk, brown sugar, and tomato paste.
- Pour pan mixture over the beans and stir well.
- Cover slow cooker and cook on low for 8 hours.
- Serve and enjoy.

Calories 485, Fat 13 g, Carbohydrates 70.4 g, Sugar 7.4 g, Protein 22.9 g, Cholesterol 0 mg

Red Beans with Bell Pepper

Total Time: 5 hours 10 minutes

Serves: 4

3/4 cup celery, chopped
1 tsp dried thyme
1 tsp paprika
3/4 tsp ground red pepper
1/2 tsp ground black pepper
3 cups water
1 cup dried red beans

1 cup onion, chopped
1 cup green bell pepper, chopped
14 oz turkey sausage, sliced
1 bay leaf
5 garlic cloves, minced
1/2 tsp salt

- Add all ingredients into the slow cooker and stir well.
- Cover and cook on high for 5 hours.
- Stir well and serve with rice.

Calories 525, Fat 29 g, Carbohydrates 35.8 g, Sugar 4.1 g, Protein 30.8 g, Cholesterol 83 mg

Spicy Black Eyed Peas

Total Time: 6 hours 30 minutes

Serves: 10

1 lb dried black-eyed peas, rinsed and drained

1 tsp ground black pepper

1 1/2 tsp cumin

1/2 tsp cayenne pepper

1 jalapeno pepper, seeded and minced

1 red bell pepper, seeded and diced

2 garlic cloves, diced

1 onion, diced

6 cups water

Salt

- Add all ingredients into the slow cooker and stir well.
- Cover and cook on low for 6 hours.
- Serve and enjoy.

Calories 122, Fat 0.2 g, Carbohydrates 30.7 g, Sugar 2.4 g, Protein 11.4 g, Cholesterol 0 mg

Chickpea Coconut Quinoa Curry

Total Time: 4 hours 20 minutes

Serves: 8

3 cups sweet potato, peeled and cut into cubes

2 cups broccoli florets

14.5 oz can coconut milk

1/4 cup quinoa

2 garlic cloves, minced

1 tbsp ginger, grated

1 cup onion, diced

15 oz can chickpeas, drained and rinsed

28 oz can tomatoes, diced

1 tsp ground turmeric

2 tsp tamari

1 tsp chili flakes

- Add all ingredients into the slow cooker and stir well.
- Cover and cook on high for 4 hours.
- Serve and enjoy.

Calories 291, Fat 12.2 g, Carbohydrates 41.3 g, Sugar 9.3 g, Protein 7.9 g, Cholesterol 0 mg

Red Beans Cabbage Soup

Total Time: 8 hours 10 minutes

Serves: 6

15 oz can red beans, drained and rinsed
4 cups water
4 garlic cloves, minced
1 bay leaf
1 tsp dried thyme
5 oz can tomato paste

1/2 head green cabbage, chopped
1 green bell pepper, seeded and diced
1 medium onion, diced
1 medium carrots, peeled and diced
1/4 tsp black pepper
Salt

- Add all ingredients into the slow cooker and stir well.
- Cover and cook on high for 8 hours.
- Stir well and serve.

Calories 275, Fat 0.9 g, Carbohydrates 51.9 g, Sugar 8.6 g, Protein 18.4 g, Cholesterol 0 mg

Gluten Free Chickpea Curry

Total Time: 4 hours 10 minutes

Serves: 4

14 oz can chickpeas, drained
3 cup sweet potatoes, peeled and chopped
1/2 tsp chili flakes
1 tbsp honey
1 tsp ground cumin
2 tsp ground turmeric

2 tsp garam masala
13 oz can cream
1 tsp vegetable oil
1 tbsp fresh ginger, grated
4 garlic cloves, minced
1 large onion, chopped

- Heat oil in the pan over medium heat.
- Add onion, garlic, and ginger to the pan and sauté for 5 minutes.
- Add onion mixture into the blender along with honey, spices, cream, and salt and blend until smooth.
- Add remaining ingredients and curry blend into the slow cooker and stir well.
- Cover and cook on high for 4 hours.
- Serve and enjoy.

Calories 636, Fat 17.9 g, Carbohydrates 113.6 g, Sugar 54.1 g, Protein 8.7 g, Cholesterol 0 mg

Vegetarian Chili Bowl

Total Time: 4 hours 20 minutes

Serves: 8

1 tsp garam masala
4 large tomatoes, peeled, seeded and chopped
1/3 cup can black beans, drained and rinsed
1/3 cup can chickpea, rinsed and drained
1 1/2 cups onions, chopped
1 cup green bell peppers, chopped
3 garlic cloves, minced
1/3 cup can red beans, rinsed and drained
1 1/2 cup vegetable stock

2 tbsp fresh cilantro, chopped
2 tbsp vegetable oil
2 green chili, minced
1/2 medium zucchini, cut into pieces
1 cup celery, chopped
1/2 tbsp chili powder
1/2 tbsp ground coriander
1/2 tsp cumin powder
1 tsp dried oregano
1 tsp dried thyme
1 tsp fresh ginger
1/4 tsp turmeric
1 1/4 tsp salt

- Heat oil in the pan over medium heat.
- Add onion, celery, green chilies, and ginger into the pan and sauté for 5 minutes.
- Add spices and stir for another 2 minutes.
- Add remaining all ingredients into the slow cooker along with pan mixture. stir well.
- Cover and cook on low for 8 hours.
- Serve and enjoy.

Calories 135, Fat 5.7 g, Carbohydrates 19.5 g, Sugar 6.7 g, Protein 4.4 g, Cholesterol 0 mg

Healthy Turmeric Lentil Bean Chili

Total Time: 4 hours 15 minutes

Serves: 6

15 oz can red beans, rinsed and drained
1 cup coconut milk
1 tsp turmeric
1 tsp chili powder
1 tsp ground cumin

6 oz can tomato paste
2 cups water
32 oz vegetable stock
1 small onion, chopped
2 cups green lentils, rinsed and drained

- Add all ingredients except coconut milk into the slow cooker and stir well.
- Cover and cook on high for 4 hours.
- Add coconut milk and stir well.
- Stir well and serve.

Calories 598, Fat 11.5 g, Carbohydrates 92.6 g, Sugar 9.2 g, Protein 35.5 g, Cholesterol 0 mg

Chickpea Kale Sweet Potato Stew

Total Time: 4 hours 20 minutes

Serves: 8

15.5 oz can chickpeas, drained and rinsed

5 oz kale, chopped

2 red bell peppers, diced

1 1/2 lbs sweet potatoes, peeled and cut into pieces

2 tbsp curry powder

1 tsp fresh ginger, peeled and minced

3 garlic cloves, minced

2 cups vegetable broth

14.5 oz can tomatoes, drained and diced

1/4 tsp black pepper

14 oz can coconut milk

1 tsp vegetable oil

1 large onion, diced

1 tbsp kosher salt

- Heat oil in the pan over medium heat.
- Add onion and 1 tsp salt and sauté for 5 minutes.
- Add potatoes and 1 tsp salt and sauté for another 5 minutes.
- Add curry powder, garlic, and ginger and stir for 2 minutes.
- Add pan mixture into the slow cooker along with remaining ingredients except for kale and coconut milk.
- Cover and cook on high for 4 hours.
- Add coconut milk and kale and stir well. Cook for another 10 minutes.
- Serve and enjoy.

Calories 323, Fat 12.6 g, Carbohydrates 47.7 g, Sugar 4.7 g, Protein 8 g, Cholesterol 0 mg

Chickpea Spinach Cauliflower Curry

Total Time: 6 hours 15 minutes

Serves: 6

2 cups baby spinach, chopped
15 oz can chickpeas
1/2 tbsp curry powder
1 tbsp garam masala
1 cup vegetable broth
14 oz can coconut milk
1 sweet potato, peeled and diced

2 cups cauliflower florets
2 cups can tomatoes, chopped
1 tbsp ginger, minced
1 garlic clove, minced
1/2 onion, chopped
1 tsp vegetable oil
1 tsp salt

- Heat oil in the pan over medium heat.
- Add ginger, garlic, and onion to the pan and sauté for 5 minutes.
- Add pan mixture into the slow cooker with remaining ingredients except for spinach.
- Cover and cook on low for 6 hours.
- Add spinach and stir well.
- Serve with rice and enjoy.

Calories 282, Fat 16.1 g, Carbohydrates 30.1 g, Sugar 5.3 g, Protein 8 g, Cholesterol 0 mg

Spicy Winter Chickpeas

Total Time: 6 hours 15 minutes

Serves: 4

1 1/2 cups dried chickpeas, rinsed and drained
2 tbsp parsley, chopped
1 tbsp lemon juice
1 bay leaf
1/2 butternut squash, cut into 1-inch cubes
10 green olive, pitted
1 tsp tamarind paste
2 garlic cloves, minced

2 tomatoes, diced
1 large onion, chopped
2 tbsp vegetable oil
1/2 tsp ground black pepper
1 tsp curry powder
1 tsp ground ginger
1 tsp garam masala
1 tsp smoked paprika
1 tsp turmeric
1/2 tsp salt

- Heat oil in the pan over medium heat.
- Add garlic, ginger, and onion to the pan and sauté for 5 minutes.
- Add spices and sauté for 1 minute. Transfer mixture into the slow cooker.
- Add remaining ingredients into the slow cooker and stir well.
- Cover and cook on low for 6 hours.
- Serve and enjoy.

Calories 425, Fat 14.3 g, Carbohydrates 60.5 g, Sugar 12.6 g, Protein 16.3 g, Cholesterol 0 mg

Spicy Curried Chickpeas

Total Time: 6 hours 20 minutes

Serves: 4

1.1 lbs chickpeas, rinsed and drained	14 oz tomatoes, chopped
1/2 tsp dried herbs	2 garlic cloves, minced
1/2 tsp nutmeg	2 onion, chopped
1/2 tsp garam masala	1 tsp cumin seeds
1/2 tsp coriander powder	4 tsp vegetable oil
1 tsp tomato puree	2 bay leaves
	Salt

- Soaked chickpeas in a water for overnight.
- Heat oil in the pan over medium heat.
- Add cumin seeds, garlic, and onion into the pan and sauté for 5 minutes.
- Add tomato paste, tomatoes and spices and sauté for 2 minutes. Transfer pan mixture into the blender and blend until smooth.
- Add chickpeas, bay leaves, and blended puree into the slow cooker and stir well.
- Cover and cook on low for 6 hours.
- Serve with rice and enjoy.

Calories 540, Fat 12.6 g, Carbohydrates 85.7 g, Sugar 18.5 g, Protein 25.8 g, Cholesterol 0 mg

Spiced Green Peas Rice

Total Time: 2 hours 20 minutes

Serves: 6

1 cup green peas
2 tsp chili powder
2 tomatoes, pureed
1 tsp turmeric powder
2 green chilies, chopped
1 tsp cumin seeds

1 tbsp vegetable oil
2 potatoes, peeled and chopped
1 cup basmati rice, rinsed and drained
2 cups water

- Add water, rice, and potatoes into the slow cooker.
- Heat oil in the pan over medium heat.
- Add cumin seeds, turmeric, chili powder, tomato puree, green chilies, and salt to the pan and sauté for 2 minutes.
- Transfer pan mixture into the slow cooker and stir well.
- Cover and cook on high for 1 1/2 hours.
- Add green peas and cook for another 30 minutes.
- Serve and enjoy.

Calories 214, Fat 3 g, Carbohydrates 41.8 g, Sugar 3.4 g, Protein 5.3 g, Cholesterol 0 mg

Buttered Peas Rice

Total Time: 2 hours 15 minutes

Serves: 4

1 cup brown rice, uncooked

2 tbsp green onion, sliced

1 cup frozen peas

1 bell pepper, chopped

2 tbsp butter

1 1/4 cup water

Pepper

Salt

- Add all ingredients into the slow cooker and mix well.
- Cover and cook on high for 2 hours.
- Serve and enjoy.

Calories 265, Fat 7.2 g, Carbohydrates 44.4 g, Sugar 3.4 g, Protein 6 g, Cholesterol 15 mg

VEGETABLE RECIPES

Delicious Spiced Potatoes and Cauliflower

Total Time: 4 hours 15 minutes

Serves: 8

1 large cauliflower head, cut into florets
1 large potato, peeled and diced
1 tsp fresh ginger, grated
2 cloves garlic, minced
2 jalapeno peppers, sliced
1 medium onion, peeled and diced
1 medium tomato, diced

1 tbsp cumin seeds
1 tsp turmeric
3 tbsp vegetable oil
1 tbsp fresh cilantro, chopped
1/4 tsp cayenne pepper
1 tbsp garam masala
1 tbsp kosher salt

- Add all ingredients except cilantro into the slow cooker and mix well.
- Cover and cook on low for 4 hours.
- Garnish with cilantro and serve.

Calories 123, Fat 5.6 g, Carbohydrates 16.7 g, Sugar 4 g, Protein 3.6 g, Cholesterol 0 mg

Scrumptious Spinach Paneer

Total Time: 5 hours 15 minutes

Serves: 6

12 oz paneer cheese
8 oz fresh spinach, chopped
30 oz frozen spinach, thawed
14 oz can coconut milk
1/8 tsp cayenne pepper
1 tbsp ground cumin

1 tbsp ground coriander
1 tbsp garam masala
1 1/2 cups can tomato sauce
3 tbsp fresh ginger, minced
4 garlic cloves, chopped
1 tsp salt

- Add all ingredients except fresh spinach and paneer into the slow cooker.
- Cover and cook on low for 3 hours.
- Add fresh spinach and cook for 1 hour.
- Using immersion blender blend mixture until smooth.
- Add paneer cheese and cook for 1 hour.
- Serve and enjoy.

Calories 220, Fat 10 g, Carbohydrates 16 g, Sugar 6 g, Protein 20 g, Cholesterol 0 mg

Tasty Spinach Potato

Total Time: 3 hours 15 minutes

Serves: 4

1 1/2 lbs potatoes, peel and cut into chunks
1/2 lb fresh spinach, chopped
1/2 tsp chili powder
1/2 tsp garam masala
1/2 tsp ground coriander

1/2 tsp cumin
1 tbsp vegetable oil
1/4 cup water
1/2 onion, sliced
Pepper
Salt

- Add all ingredients into the slow cooker and stir well.
- Cover and cook on low for 3 hours.
- Serve and enjoy.

Calories 168, Fat 3.9 g, Carbohydrates 30.4 g, Sugar 2.8 g, Protein 4.7 g, Cholesterol 0 mg

Spicy Eggplant Potatoes

Total Time: 2 hours 40 minutes

Serves: 8

2 medium eggplants, cut into 1-inch cubes
1 large potato, peeled and cut into 1/2 inch cubes
2 jalapeño chilies, seeded and minced
1 tbsp ground cumin
1 tbsp chili powder

1 medium onion, chopped
1 tsp ginger, grated
6 garlic cloves, minced
1 tbsp garam masala
1 tsp turmeric
2 tbsp fresh cilantro, chopped
1/4 cup vegetable oil
1 tbsp kosher salt

- Add all ingredients into the slow cooker and stir well.
- Cover and cook on high for 2 hours.
- Remove lid and cook on low for another 30 minutes.
- Serve and enjoy.

Calories 147, Fat 7.5 g, Carbohydrates 19.4 g, Sugar 5.2 g, Protein 2.9 g, Cholesterol 0 mg

Healthy Vegetable Coconut Curry

Total Time: 4 hours 20 minutes

Serves: 8

1/4 cup cilantro, chopped
1 cup green peas
1 1/2 cups carrots, peeled and cut into strips
14 oz can coconut milk
1 oz dry onion soup mix
2 bell pepper, cut into strips
1/2 tsp cayenne pepper

1/2 tsp red pepper flakes
1 tbsp chili powder
2 tbsp flour
1/4 cup curry powder
5 potatoes, peeled and cut into cubes
Water as needed

- Add all ingredients into the slow cooker and mix well.
- Cover and cook on low for 4 hours.
- Stir well and serve.

Calories 370, Fat 18.3 g, Carbohydrates 48.8 g, Sugar 5.4 g, Protein 8.2 g, Cholesterol 0 mg

Easy Whole Cauliflower Curry

Total Time: 4 hours 15 minutes

Serves: 4

1 large cauliflower head, trimmed
2 garlic cloves, sliced
1/2 onion, chopped
2 small potatoes, quartered
1 red pepper, sliced
For sauce:

1/2 tsp cayenne pepper
1 tsp cumin
2 tbsp curry powder
2 cups can coconut milk
2 cups vegetable broth

- Add red pepper, potatoes, onion, garlic, and cauliflower into the slow cooker.
- In a bowl, whisk together all sauce ingredients and pour over cauliflower.
- Cover and cook on low for 4 hours.
- About 15 minutes before serving add coconut milk and stir well.
- Serve and enjoy.

Calories 383, Fat 25.8 g, Carbohydrates 34.3 g, Sugar 8.6 g, Protein 11.4 g, Cholesterol 0 mg

Vegetable Curried Rice

Total Time: 4 hours 10 minutes
Serves: 4

1 1/2 cups green cabbage, chopped
2 cups mushrooms, chopped
1 cup broccoli, chopped
1 cup brown rice
1 tsp curry powder
2 tbsp apple cider vinegar

1/4 tsp dried thyme
1/2 tsp garlic powder
1/2 tsp black pepper
4 cups vegetable broth
1 tsp salt

- Add all ingredients into the slow cooker and mix well.
- Cover and cook on low for 4 hours.
- Using fork fluff the rice.
- Serve and enjoy.

Calories 237, Fat 2.9 g, Carbohydrates 42.1 g, Sugar 2.7 g, Protein 10.7 g, Cholesterol 0 mg

Curried Zucchini Eggplant

Total Time: 4 hours 15 minutes

Serves: 4

4 cups zucchini, chopped
4 cups eggplant, peeled and
chopped
1/4 cup vegetable broth
15 oz can coconut milk
6 oz can tomato paste
1/4 tsp cumin

1/4 tsp cayenne pepper
1 tbsp garam masala
1 tbsp curry powder
4 garlic cloves, minced
1 onion, chopped
1 tsp salt

- Add all ingredients into the slow cooker and mix well.
- Cover and cook on low for 4 hours.
- Stir well and serve with rice.

Calories 307, Fat 23.6 g, Carbohydrates 24.3 g, Sugar 10.9 g, Protein 7.2 g, Cholesterol 0 mg

Flavourful Vegetable Korma

Total Time: 5 hours 15 minutes

Serves: 4

2 tbsp almond meal
1 tbsp red pepper flakes
1 tsp garam masala
2 tbsp curry powder
10 oz coconut milk
2 garlic cloves, minced
1/2 large onion, chopped

1 cup green beans, chopped
1/2 cup frozen green peas
2 large carrots, chopped
1 large cauliflower head, cut into florets
1 tsp sea salt

- Add all ingredients into the slow cooker and stir well.
- Cover and cook on high for 5 hours.
- Serve and enjoy.

Calories 295, Fat 19.4 g, Carbohydrates 28.7 g, Sugar 11.8 g, Protein 9.1 g, Cholesterol 0 mg

Potato Okra Curry

Total Time: 3 hours 15 minutes

Serves: 6

1 1/2 lbs potatoes, peeled and cut into pieces
1 lb okra, cut the ends and sliced
2 cups vegetable stock
13 oz can coconut milk
1 1/2 tbsp curry powder
3/4 tsp red pepper flakes

2 tsp fresh ginger, grated
4 garlic cloves, minced
1 large onion, chopped
1 1/2 tbsp vegetable oil
1 bell pepper, seeded and chopped
1 1/2 tsp salt

- Add potatoes, bell pepper, and okra into the slow cooker.
- Heat oil in a pan over medium heat.
- Add garlic, onion, and ginger to the pan and sauté for 5 minutes.
- Remove pan from heat and stir in spices.
- Transfer pan mixture into the slow cooker and stir well.
- Cover and cook on low for 3 hours.
- Stir well and serve with rice.

Calories 290, Fat 17.8 g, Carbohydrates 31.8 g, Sugar 5.3 g, Protein 5.5 g, Cholesterol 0 mg

Delicious Navratan Korma

Total Time: 8 hours 15 minutes

Serves: 4

1 cup cauliflower florets	1/2 tsp ground coriander
1/2 cup tomatoes, diced	1/2 tsp ground turmeric
1/2 cup green peas	1 tbsp ginger, grated
1 cup carrots, chopped	2 tbsp bell pepper, minced
2 tbsp sour cream	1/4 onion, chopped
1/4 cup coconut milk	1/2 cup water
1 tbsp raisins	Salt
1/4 tsp chili powder	

- Add all ingredients except sour cream into the slow cooker and stir well.
- Cover and cook on low for 8 hours.
- Stir in sour cream and serve with rice.

Calories 118, Fat 5.3 g, Carbohydrates 16.8 g, Sugar 8.8 g, Protein 3.4 g, Cholesterol 3 mg

Slow Cooker Sambar

Total Time: 6 hours 10 minutes

Serves: 2

1/4 cup pink lentils
1 cup water
1/2 tsp tamarind paste
1 tsp sambar powder
4 curry leaves
1/4 cup tomatoes, chopped

1/4 cup eggplants, cut into pieces
1/4 cup pumpkin, cut into pieces
1 medium onion, sliced
1 drumstick, peeled and cut into pieces
Salt

- Add all ingredients into the slow cooker and stir well.
- Cover and cook on low for 6 hours.
- Stir well and serve hot with rice.

Calories 130, Fat 0.6 g, Carbohydrates 24.7 g, Sugar 5.3 g, Protein 7.5 g, Cholesterol 0 mg

Creamy Carrot Squash Soup

Total Time: 6 hours 15 minutes

Serves: 8

1 lb butternut squash, peeled and diced
1/2 lb carrots, peeled and cut into chunks
13.5 oz can coconut milk
1/4 tsp ground sage

1 tsp pepper
1 bay leaf
3 cups vegetable broth
1 apple, peeled and sliced
1 medium onion, diced
1 tsp salt

- Add squash, bay leaf, apple, carrots, onion, and broth into the slow cooker.
- Cover and cook on low for 6 hours.
- Discard bay leaf and using immersion blender blend until smooth.
- Add coconut milk, sage, pepper, and salt. Stir well.
- Serve and enjoy.

Calories 163, Fat 11.3 g, Carbohydrates 15.8 g, Sugar 5.1 g, Protein 3.8 g, Cholesterol 0 mg

Yummy Slow Cooked Potatoes

Total Time: 6 hours 15 minutes

Serves: 4

2.2 lbs potatoes, peel and cut into cubes
1/2 tsp chili powder
1/2 tsp cumin
1 1/2 tsp turmeric
1 tsp garam masala

1 tsp ground ginger
1 tsp mustard seeds
4 tomatoes, chopped
1/4 tsp red chili flakes
1 tbsp vegetable oil
1 tsp salt

- In a bowl, mix together chili flakes, chili powder, cumin, turmeric, garam masala, and ginger.
- Heat oil in the pan over medium heat.
- Add mustard seeds into the pan and stir until they start to pop then add onion and sauté until lightly brown.
- Add mixed spices and stir for a minute.
- Add tomatoes and salt and stir for a minute.
- Place potatoes in the slow cooker then pour pan mixture over the potatoes.
- Cover and cook on low for 6 hours.
- Stir well and serve.

Calories 235, Fat 4.4 g, Carbohydrates 45.8 g, Sugar 6.2 g, Protein 5.7 g, Cholesterol 0 mg

Curried Potatoes

Total Time: 6 hours 15 minutes

Serves: 6

7 potatoes, washed and cut into chunks
2 tsp sugar
2 tsp chili powder
2 tsp curry powder

2 tsp paprika
14.5 oz can tomatoes, diced
1 tbsp vegetable oil
1/2 tsp kosher salt

- Add all ingredients into the slow cooker and stir well.
- Cover and cook on low for 6 hours.
- Serve and enjoy.

Calories 218, Fat 2.9 g, Carbohydrates 45.1 g, Sugar 6.7 g, Protein 5.1 g, Cholesterol 0 mg

Mushroom Eggplant Potato Curry

Total Time: 4 hours 15 minutes

Serves: 6

8 mushrooms, quartered
1 large eggplant, peeled and cut into
1-inch pieces
3 potatoes, peeled and cut into 1/2
inch cubes
1 bay leaf
2 tsp fresh ginger, grated
14 oz can tomatoes, chopped

1/2 cup red pepper, chopped
1 tsp black pepper
1 tbsp ground cumin
2 garlic cloves, minced
1 large onion, chopped
2 tbsp vegetable oil
1 tsp lime juice
Salt

- Heat oil in the pan over medium heat.
- Add eggplant to the pan and sauté until lightly brown.
- Transfer eggplant to the slow cooker.
- In the same pan, add onion and sauté for 3 minutes. Add garlic, pepper, and cumin and sauté for a minute.
- Transfer onion mixture to the slow cooker along with remaining all ingredients and stir well.
- Cover and cook on high for 4 hours.
- Stir well and serve.

Calories 173, Fat 5.3 g, Carbohydrates 29.4 g, Sugar 6.7 g, Protein 4.6 g, Cholesterol 0 mg

Eggplant Chickpea Curry

Total Time: 8 hours 40 minutes

Serves: 6

15 oz can chickpeas, rinsed and drained
1 tbsp fresh ginger, minced
2 tsp cumin
1 tbsp garam masala
1 tbsp curry powder

3 cups vegetable broth
15 oz can tomatoes
4 garlic cloves, minced
3 lbs eggplant, diced
2 cups onion, diced
2 tsp salt

- Add all ingredients except chickpeas into the slow cooker.
- Cover and cook on low for 8 hours.
- Add chickpeas and cook for another 30 minutes.
- Stir well and serve.

Calories 203, Fat 2.3 g, Carbohydrates 39.2 g, Sugar 11.3 g, Protein 9.7 g, Cholesterol 0 mg

Coconut Eggplant Curry

Total Time: 4 hours 10 minutes

Serves: 6

2 lbs eggplant, cut into 1 inch cubed
4 garlic cloves, minced
14.5 oz can coconut milk
6 oz tomato paste
1 tbsp curry powder
1 medium onion, chopped

1 green bell pepper, seeded and chopped
2 Serrano peppers, seeded and minced
1 tbsp garam masala
1 tsp salt

- Add all ingredients into the slow cooker and stir well.
- Cover and cook on low for 4 hours.
- Serve and enjoy.

Calories 216, Fat 15.2 g, Carbohydrates 20.7 g, Sugar 9.8 g, Protein 4.8 g, Cholesterol 0 mg

Creamy Cauliflower Soup

Total Time: 4 hours 20 minutes

Serves: 6

1 cauliflower head	5.3 oz plain yogurt
2 cups vegetable broth	1 tbsp curry powder
3 garlic cloves	1 tbsp water
1/4 cup dried cranberries	3/4 tsp garam masala
1/4 cup pine nuts	1/2 cup sugar
13.5 oz can coconut milk	1/2 tsp salt

- Add cauliflower, broth, and garlic into the slow cooker. Cover and cook on low for 4 hours.
- Add cauliflower mixture into the blender along with yogurt and coconut milk and blend until smooth.
- Pour into the six serving bowls.
- In a pan, cook over medium heat pine nuts with water, garam masala, and sugar. Cook until sugar is crystallized.
- Sprinkle pan mixture over the soup.
- Serve and enjoy.

Calories 276, Fat 18.5 g, Carbohydrates 25.1 g, Sugar 20.1 g, Protein 6.2 g, Cholesterol 2 mg

Delicious Sweet Potato Curry

Total Time: 6 hours 15 minutes

Serves: 6

1 sweet potato, diced
1 courgette, diced
1/4 cup cashew nuts
14 oz can tomatoes, chopped
1 tsp curry powder
1/2 tsp chili powder
1/2 tsp black pepper
2 tbsp tomato puree

4 tbsp flour
14 oz can coconut milk
1 tsp garlic, minced
2 onions, diced
4 tomatoes, diced
1 tsp ginger, minced
2 tsp garam masala
1 tbsp vegetable oil

- Heat oil in the pan over medium heat.
- Add ginger, onion, and garlic to the pan and sauté for 5 minutes.
- Add tomato paste, flour, and spices and cook for a minute.
- Add coconut milk and stir well and cook until thickened.
- Transfer pan mixture into the slow cooker along with remaining ingredients and mix well.
- Cover and cook on low for 6 hours.
- Serve and enjoy.

Calories 275, Fat 19.5 g, Carbohydrates 24 g, Sugar 8.3 g, Protein 5.5 g, Cholesterol 0 mg

Flavorful Vegetable Curry

Total Time: 7 hours 15 minutes

Serves: 4

15 oz can chickpeas, rinsed and drained
8 oz fresh green beans, cut into 1-inch pieces
4 medium carrots, sliced
2 medium potatoes, cut into 1/2 inch cubes
1 cup onion, chopped
14 oz can vegetable broth

14 oz can tomatoes, diced
2 tbsp tapioca
2 tsp curry powder
1 tsp ground coriander
3 garlic cloves, minced
1/8 tsp ground cinnamon
1/4 tsp red pepper, crushed
1/4 tsp salt

- Add all ingredients into the slow cooker and stir well.
- Cover and cook on low for 7 hours.
- Stir well and serve with rice.

Calories 367, Fat 3.1 g, Carbohydrates 75.3 g Sugar 11.8 g, Protein 12.6 g, Cholesterol 1 mg

Delicious Tofu Coconut Curry

Total Time: 4 hours 15 minutes

Serves: 4

1 cup firm tofu, diced	1 tbsp garam masala
2 tsp garlic cloves, minced	2 tbsp butter
1 cup onion, chopped	1 tbsp curry powder
8 oz tomato paste	10 oz can coconut milk
2 cups bell pepper, chopped	1 1/2 tsp sea salt

- Add all ingredients into the slow cooker and stir well.
- Cover and cook on low for 4 hours.
- Stir well and serve with rice.

Calories 179, Fat 9.1 g, Carbohydrates 20.4 g, Sugar 11.6 g, Protein 8.9 g, Cholesterol 15 mg

Creamy Coconut Pumpkin Curry

Total Time: 6 hours 15 minutes

Serves: 6

15 oz can coconut milk, unsweetened

2 cups pumpkin puree

1 cup vegetable stock

3 carrots, cut into 1-inch pieces

3 cups sweet potatoes, cut into 1-inch cubes

1/2 tbsp curry powder

1/4 tsp turmeric powder

1/4 tsp ground black pepper

1/2 large onion, diced

1 garlic clove, minced

2 chicken breasts, cut into 1-inch cubes

1 lime juice

2 tsp garam masala

1/2 tsp kosher salt

- Add all ingredients into the slow cooker and mix well.
- Cover and cook on low for 6 hours.
- Serve with rice and enjoy.

Calories 357, Fat 17.7 g, Carbohydrates 35 g, Sugar 7.4 g, Protein 17.6 g, Cholesterol 43 mg

Hearty Potato Curry

Total Time: 8 hours 10 minutes

Serves: 4

1 lb potatoes, cut into 1-inch cubes
1/2 tsp cumin
1/2 tsp coriander
1/2 tsp peppercorns
1 cinnamon stick
1 cups vegetable stock
1 tsp tamarind paste
1 bay leaf
1/4 tsp red pepper, crushed
1/2 tsp garam masala
4 garlic cloves, minced

2 tsp ginger, minced
1 onion, diced
2 tbsp vegetable oil
1 1/2 tsp paprika
1 1/2 tsp turmeric
1/2 cup frozen peas
2 cups coconut milk
2 tbsp all purpose flour
Pepper
Salt

- Heat 1 tbsp oil in the pan over medium heat.
- Add onion and cook until golden brown, about 3 minutes.
- Add powder spices and stir for 1 minute.
- Transfer onion mixture to the blender with tamarind, ginger, garlic, and coconut milk and blend until smooth.
- Pour blended mixture into the slow cooker with remaining ingredients except for peas and flour.
- Cover and cook on low for 8 hours.
- Add peas and stir well. Whisk flour in little water and pour into the slow cooker.
- Stir well and serve.

Calories 476, Fat 36.5 g, Carbohydrates 37.2 g, Sugar 8.8 g, Protein 7 g, Cholesterol 0 mg

Mix Vegetable Curry

Total Time: 6 hours 10 minutes

Serves: 4

3 1/2 cups broccoli florets
2.5 oz green beans
2 medium carrots, peeled and sliced
2 large sweet potatoes, diced
3 tbsp tomato puree
14 oz can coconut milk
1 red chili, seeded and chopped
1 tsp garam masala

1 tsp ground turmeric
2 tsp ground coriander
2 tsp ground cumin
1 tsp chili powder
1 tsp ginger, grated
1 tsp garlic, grated
1 onion, diced

- Add all ingredients except green beans into the slow cooker and mix well.
- Cover and cook on low for 5 hours.
- Add green beans and stir well and cook for another 1 hour.
- Serve with rice.

Calories 313, Fat 22 g, Carbohydrates 28.3 g, Sugar 5.1 g, Protein 6.3 g, Cholesterol 0 mg

MEAT RECIPES

Tasty Chicken Tikka Masala

Total Time: 6 hours 25 minutes

Serves: 6

2 lbs chicken thighs, skinless and boneless, cut into 2-inch pieces
10 oz frozen peas, thawed
1 1/2 cups heavy cream
1 tbsp cornstarch
1 tbsp sugar
28 oz can tomatoes
1 tsp ginger, grated
3 tbsp garam masala

1/2 tsp red pepper flakes
6 garlic cloves, minced
1 large onion, diced
2 tbsp vegetable oil
1 cup plain yogurt
1 tbsp ground cumin
1 tbsp ground coriander
1 tsp kosher salt

- In a large bowl, combine together chicken, yogurt, cumin, ground coriander, and salt. Marinade for 10 minutes.
- Heat 1 tbsp oil in the pan over medium-high heat.
- Place marinated chicken into the pan and cook until lightly brown on both the sides.
- Transfer chicken into the slow cooker.
- In the same pan, heat remaining oil. Add onions, red pepper flakes, and garlic and saute for 5 minutes.
- Add ginger, garam masala, and salt and cook for 1 minute.
- Add sugar and tomatoes, turn heat to high and bring to boil. Transfer into the slow cooker.
- Cover and cook on low for 6 hours.
- Whisk together 1/4 cup heavy cream and cornstarch and add to the slow cooker along with remaining peas and heavy cream.
- Stir to mix and cover and cook for another 10 minutes.
- Serve and enjoy.

Calories 557, Fat 27.8 g, Carbohydrates 24.5 g, Sugar 12.7 g, Protein 51.1 g, Cholesterol 178 mg

Delicious Chicken Tandoori

Total Time: 8 hours 20 minutes

Serves: 4

14 oz coconut milk
4 chicken thighs
1 tsp fresh ginger, grated
1 tsp paprika
1 tsp cayenne pepper

2 tsp tomato paste
2 tsp garam masala
1 tsp ground coriander
1 tsp ground cumin

- Add all ingredients into the slow cooker and mix well.
- Cover and cook on low for 8 hours.
- Serve and enjoy.

Calories 514, Fat 34.8 g, Carbohydrates 7.1 g, Sugar 3.8 g, Protein 44.9 g, Cholesterol 130 mg

Peanut Butter Chicken

Total Time: 4 hours 30 minutes

Serves: 6

3 chicken breasts, skinless and boneless
1 tbsp lime juice
2 tbsp cornstarch
3 garlic cloves, minced
1 tbsp ginger, minced

1 tbsp rice wine vinegar
2 tbsp honey
2 tbsp soy sauce
1/3 cup creamy peanut butter
1 cup coconut milk

- Add all ingredients except lime juice and cornstarch into the slow cooker and mix well.
- Cover and cook on low for 4 hours.
- Whisk together cornstarch and 2 tbsp water and pour into the slow cooker.
- Stir well and cook for another 20 minutes until gravy thickens.
- Serve and enjoy.

Calories 356, Fat 22.2 g, Carbohydrates 15.4 g, Sugar 8.7 g, Protein 26.2 g, Cholesterol 65 mg

Spicy Chicken Curry

Total Time: 6 hours 20 minutes

Serves: 4

4 chicken thighs, boneless and cut into chunks
3 tbsp flour
2 tsp ground coriander
2 tsp garam masala
2 tsp turmeric
2 tsp ground cumin
1 tsp ginger, grated
1/2 lemon juice
4 garlic cloves, crushed
2 onion, chopped
2 green chilies, chopped
14 oz can tomatoes, chopped
1 tbsp vegetable oil

- Add ginger, chilies, garlic, and onion into the blender and blend until smooth.
- Heat oil in the pan over medium heat.
- Add blended puree into the pan and sauté for 3 minutes.
- Add spices and sauté for 2-3 minutes.
- Add flour and tomatoes into the pan and stir well.
- Refill tomato can halfway with water and adds in the pan. Stir well.
- Add chicken into the slow cooker and season with pepper and salt.
- Pour pan mixture over the chicken with lemon juice.
- Cover and cook on low for 6 hours.
- Serve and enjoy.

Calories 387, Fat 14.8 g, Carbohydrates 17.3 g, Sugar 6 g, Protein 44.9 g, Cholesterol 130 mg

Juicy and Tender Goat Curry

Total Time: 5 hours 15 minutes

Serves: 6

2 lbs goat meat

2 Serrano pepper, minced

1 tsp paprika

1 tsp chili powder

1 tsp turmeric powder

1 tsp cumin powder

1 tbsp coriander powder

2 cardamom pods

2 garlic cloves, minced

1 tbsp ghee

1 bay leaf

3 whole cloves

1 tsp fresh ginger, minced

1 large onion, chopped

1 cup water

1 tsp garam masala

28 oz can tomatoes, diced

2 tsp salt

- Add cardamom and cloves into the grinder and grind well.
- Add all ingredients into the slow cooker except water, garam masala, and tomatoes.
- Cover and cook on high for 4 hours.
- Add water, garam masala, and tomatoes and stir well.
- Cook for another 1 hour until meat is tender.
- Serve and enjoy.

Calories 230, Fat 5.9 g, Carbohydrates 10.6 g, Sugar 5.8 g, Protein 33.6 g, Cholesterol 92 mg

Delicious Slow Cooked Beef

Total Time: 6 hours 15 minutes

Serves: 4

2 lbs beef chuck steak, diced
1/2 cup coriander, chopped
2 cardamom pods
1 cinnamon stick
14 oz can tomatoes, diced
1/4 cup curry paste

1 red chili, chopped
1 tsp ginger, grated
2 garlic cloves, crushed
1 large onion, sliced
2 tbsp vegetable oil
1/4 cup plain flour

- Add beef and flour into the ziplock bag and shake well.
- Heat oil in the saucepan over medium heat.
- Add beef into the saucepan and cook for 3-4 minutes or until lightly brown. Transfer beef into the slow cooker.
- In the same pan, add onion, ginger, and garlic and sauté for 4 minutes.
- Add curry paste and chili and stir for 1 minute.
- Add 3/4 cup water, tomatoes, cardamom, and cinnamon and stir well. Transfer mixture into the slow cooker.
- Cover and cook on low for 5 1/2 hours or until beef is tender.
- Add coriander and stir well.
- Serve and enjoy.

Calories 651, Fat 29.9 g, Carbohydrates 19.7 g, Sugar 5 g, Protein 71.8 g, Cholesterol 203 mg

Simple Beef Curry

Total Time: 8 hours 40 minutes

Serves: 4

12 oz beef steak, cut into 1-inch pieces
2 onions, chopped
14 oz can tomatoes, chopped
2 tsp garam masala
4 garlic cloves, chopped
4 tsp ground cumin
4 tsp ground coriander
2 tsp ground turmeric
2 chilies, chopped
1 tsp ginger, grated
7 oz yogurt
4 tbsp vegetable oil

- Heat oil in the pan over medium heat.
- Add beef to the pan and cook for 4-5 minutes or until lightly brown. Transfer beef into the slow cooker.
- In the same pan, sauté onion, ginger, chili, and garlic for 2 minutes.
- Add spices and stir-fry for 1 minute. Transfer pan mixture to the slow cooker.
- Add remaining ingredients except for yogurt into the slow cooker and stir well.
- Cover and cook on low for 8 hours.
- Add yogurt and stir well and cook for another 30 minutes.
- Serve and enjoy.

Calories 375, Fat 20.2 g, Carbohydrates 16.7 g, Sugar 9.3 g, Protein 30.8 g, Cholesterol 79 mg

Easy Curried Chicken

Total Time: 4 hours 15 minutes

Serves: 4

2 tbsp tomato paste	1 cinnamon stick
14 oz can coconut milk	2 bay leaves
3 garlic cloves, minced	1 1/2 lbs chicken thighs
2 tbsp fresh ginger, minced	1 medium onion, diced
1 tsp cumin	1/4 cup fresh cilantro, chopped
1 tsp turmeric	1 1/2 tsp salt
1 tsp garam masala	

- Add all ingredients into the slow cooker and stir well.
- Cover and cook on low for 4 hours.
- Using fork shred the meat and stir well into the sauce.
- Serve and enjoy.

Calories 553, Fat 34.2 g, Carbohydrates 10.2 g, Sugar 2.3 g, Protein 52.4 g, Cholesterol 151 mg

Chicken Vegetable Curry

Total Time: 3 hours 25 minutes

Serves: 4

2 cups mushrooms, sliced
1 cup green peas
3 chicken breasts, skinless, boneless and cut into pieces
2 tsp ground cayenne
1/2 tsp black pepper
3 tbsp curry powder

1 packet dry onion soup mix
14 oz can coconut milk
10.75 oz can chicken soup
10.75 oz can mushroom soup
1 onion, chopped
1 tbsp butter

- Melt butter in the pan over medium heat.
- Add onion and cook for 5 minutes. Transfer to the slow cooker.
- Add remaining ingredients and stir well.
- Cover and cook on high for 1 1/2 hours then reduce heat to low and cook for another 1 1/2 hours.
- Serve and enjoy.

Calories 635, Fat 37.9 g, Carbohydrates 32 g, Sugar 2.3 g, Protein 45.2 g, Cholesterol 111 mg

Spicy Cauliflower Chicken

Total Time: 6 hours 15 minutes

Serves: 4

1 1/2 lbs chicken thighs, skinless, boneless and cut into halves
1 small cauliflower head, cut into florets
1/4 cup raisins
1 onion, chopped

1 tbsp curry powder
2 tbsp ginger, grated
2 tbsp tomato paste
28 oz can tomatoes, diced
1/2 tsp kosher salt

- Add all ingredients into the slow cooker and stir well.
- Cover and cook on low for 6 hours.
- Serve and enjoy.

Calories 391, Fat 17.3 g, Carbohydrates 26.7 g, Sugar 6.7 g, Protein 31.1 g, Cholesterol 96 mg

Yummy Butter Chicken

Total Time: 4 hours 30 minutes

Serves: 6

4 large chicken thighs, skinless, boneless and cut into pieces
14 oz can coconut milk
1 cup plain yogurt
15 green cardamom pods
6 oz can tomato paste
1 tsp garam masala
2 tsp tandoori masala

1 tsp curry paste
2 tsp curry powder
3 garlic cloves, minced
1 onion, diced
3 tbsp vegetable oil
2 tbsp butter
Salt

- Heat butter and oil in a pan over medium heat.
- Add chicken, garlic, and onion to the pan and cook until onion softens.
- Stir in tomato paste, garam masala, tandoori masala, curry paste, and curry powder.
- Transfer chicken mixture into the slow cooker.
- Stir in yogurt, coconut milk, and cardamom pods.
- Season with salt.
- Cover and cook on high for 4 hours.
- Serve and enjoy.

Calories 480, Fat 33.3 g, Carbohydrates 17.2 g, Sugar 7.1 g, Protein 30.6 g, Cholesterol 103 mg

Lamb Curry

Total Time: 8 hours 15 minutes

Serves: 6

2 lbs lamb meat, cut into 1 1/2" cubes
1/4 cup cilantro, chopped
20 almonds
1/4 tsp saffron threads
1 cup plain yogurt
1/2 tsp turmeric
2 large onion, sliced
6 tbsp vegetable oil

3 tomatoes, chopped
1/4 cup dried coconut, unsweetened
5 garlic cloves, crushed
1 tsp fresh ginger, grated
1 tsp garam masala
1 tsp cumin seeds
3 green Chile pepper
4 dried red Chile pepper
Salt

- Add tomatoes, grated coconut, garlic, ginger, garam masala, cumin seeds, green chilies, and red chilies into the blender and blend until smooth.
- Heat oil in a pan over medium heat.
- Add onion to the pan and sauté for 5 minutes or until softened.
- Add spice paste to the pan and cook for 3 minutes.
- Stir in meat and salt. Cook over medium heat for 8 minutes.
- Mix in almonds, saffron, and yogurt until well combined.
- Transfer pan mixture into the slow cooker and stir well.
- Cover and cook on low for 8 hours.
- Serve and enjoy.

Calories 489, Fat 35.4 g, Carbohydrates 16.1 g, Sugar 7.1 g, Protein 28.1 g, Cholesterol 88 mg

Chicken Quinoa Curry

Total Time: 4 hours 45 minutes

Serves: 6

1 1/2 lbs chicken breast, diced
1/3 cup quinoa
1/4 tsp paprika
1 tbsp curry powder
1/4 cup coconut milk

1 cup chicken broth
1 3/4 cups apples, chopped
1 1/4 cups celery, chopped
3/4 cup onion, chopped

- Add all ingredients except quinoa into the slow cooker and stir well.
- Cover and cook on low for 4 hours.
- Add quinoa and stir well. Cook for another 35 minutes.
- Stir well and serve.

Calories 185, Fat 3.1 g, Carbohydrates 14.4 g, Sugar 8.2 g, Protein 24.4 g, Cholesterol 59 mg

Delicious Chicken Stew

Total Time: 4 hours 15 minutes

Serves: 8

2 lbs chicken thighs, skinless, boneless and cut into pieces
1 medium onion, chopped
3 garlic cloves, minced
1/4 tsp ground black pepper
15 oz can chickpeas, rinsed and drained
14 oz can tomatoes, diced

1 cup chicken broth
5 tsp curry powder
2 tsp ground ginger
1 bay leaf
1 tbsp vegetable oil
2 tbsp lime juice
1/2 tsp salt

- Add all ingredients into the slow cooker and mix well.
- Cover and cook on high for 4 hours.
- Serve and enjoy.

Calories 322, Fat 11.1 g, Carbohydrates 17.4 g, Sugar 2.4 g, Protein 36.9 g, Cholesterol 101 mg

Creamy Coconut Chicken Curry

Total Time: 4 hours 15 minutes

Serves: 4

1 lb chicken breasts, skinless and boneless
2 tbsp lemon juice
1 cup green peas
1/2 tsp cayenne
2 tbsp curry powder
15 oz can tomato sauce

1/2 cup chicken stock
1/2 cup coconut milk
2 medium sweet potatoes, diced
15 oz can chickpeas, drained and rinsed
1 medium onion, sliced
1 tsp salt

- Add all ingredients except peas into the slow cooker and mix well.
- Cover and cook on high for 4 hours.
- Add peas and stir well.
- Serve and enjoy.

Calories 579, Fat 17.9 g, Carbohydrates 62.4 g, Sugar 9.5 g, Protein 44.2 g, Cholesterol 101 mg

Tasty Chicken Kheema

Total Time: 4 hours 20 minutes

Serves: 4

1 lb ground chicken
3/4 cup frozen peas
1 bay leaf
3/4 tsp ground cinnamon
3/4 tsp garam masala
3/4 tsp ground turmeric
3/4 tsp chili powder
3/4 tsp ground cumin
3/4 tsp ground coriander

1 jalapeno, seeded and chopped
4 tbsp cilantro, chopped
3/4 cup can tomato sauce
1 tsp ginger, grated
3 garlic cloves, minced
1 medium onion, chopped
2 tsp butter
1 tsp kosher salt

- Heat butter in a pan over medium heat.
- Add onion to the pan and sauté for 5 minutes.
- Add ginger and garlic and sauté for 2 minutes.
- Add ground chicken and salt and cook for 5 minutes.
- Transfer chicken mixture to the slow cooker along with remaining ingredients and stir well.
- Cover and cook on high for 4 hours.
- Serve and enjoy.

Calories 291, Fat 10.8 g, Carbohydrates 11.8 g, Sugar 4.7 g, Protein 35.8 g, Cholesterol 106 mg

Shredded Lamb

Total Time: 6 hours 15 minutes

Serves: 6

4.4 lbs lamb shoulder	1 tsp ground coriander
3 tsp vegetable oil	6 peppercorns
1 cup chicken stock	1 tsp fennel seeds
1 tbsp ginger, sliced	1 bay leaf
4 garlic cloves, crushed	1 tsp cumin seeds
2 large onions, sliced	1 cinnamon stick
Spice Rub:	6 cloves
1 tsp red chili powder	1-star anise

- Add allspice rub ingredients into the grinder and grind to coarse powder.
- Rub spice powder onto the lamb from both the sides.
- Heat oil in the pan over medium-high heat.
- Place lamb onto the pan and brown them on both the sides and set aside.
- Add remaining ingredients into the slow cooker.
- Place lamb into the slow cooker.
- Cover and cook on high for 6 hours or until meat is tender.
- Remove lamb from slow cooker and using fork shred the meat.
- Return shredded meat to the slow cooker and stir well.
- Serve with rice and enjoy.

Calories 671, Fat 27.1 g, Carbohydrates 6.7 g, Sugar 2.3 g, Protein 94.4 g, Cholesterol 299 mg

Yummy Chicken Soup

Total Time: 12 hours 15 minutes

Serves: 6

3 carrots, peeled and sliced
1 tsp ginger, crushed
1/2 tsp garlic, crushed
1/4 tsp turmeric
1/2 onion, diced
12 cups water

5 cloves
2 cinnamon sticks
1/4 tsp black peppercorns
2 chicken breasts
1 lb chicken
1 tbsp sea salt

- Add all ingredients into the slow cooker.
- Cover and cook on low for 12 hours.
- Remove chicken from slow cooker and using fork shred the chicken.
- Return shredded chicken to the slow cooker and stir well.
- Season with pepper and salt.
- Serve and enjoy.

Calories 225, Fat 5.9 g, Carbohydrates 4.3 g, Sugar 1.9 g, Protein 36.4 g, Cholesterol 102 mg

Sweet Beef Curry

Total Time: 8 hours 15 minutes

Serves: 6

2.2 lbs stew beef
1 tbsp raisins
1 tbsp relish
1 tbsp tomato sauce
2 carrots, peeled and chopped
1 onion, chopped
2 celery stalks, chopped

2 apples, chopped
1 tbsp Worcestershire sauce
1/2 cup water
1 tbsp golden syrup
2 tbsp brown sugar
1 tbsp curry powder
2 tsp salt

- Add all ingredients into the slow cooker and mix well.
- Cover and cook on low for 8 hours.
- Serve and enjoy.

Calories 333, Fat 10.3 g, Carbohydrates 23 g, Sugar 15.7 g, Protein 37.4 g, Cholesterol 0 mg

Yellow Chicken Curry

Total Time: 4 hours 15 minutes

Serves: 6

1 1/2 lbs chicken thighs, boneless, skinless and cut into pieces
1 lb potatoes, diced
1 medium onion, diced
13.5 oz can coconut milk
2 tbsp brown sugar
1 tsp ground turmeric

1 tsp curry powder
2 tsp garlic, minced
1 tbsp fresh ginger, minced
1/2 tsp ground coriander seed
1/2 tsp red pepper
1 tsp kosher salt

- Add all ingredients into the slow cooker and stir well.
- Cover and cook on low for 4 hours.
- Serve and enjoy.

Calories 296, Fat 8.7 g, Carbohydrates 20.5 g, Sugar 5.1 g, Protein 35.9 g, Cholesterol 101 mg

Spinach Lamb Curry

Total Time: 4 hours 20 minutes

Serves: 8

2 cups plain yogurt
6 cups baby spinach
3 lbs lamb meat, boneless and cut into pieces
2 cups beef broth
1 1/2 tsp ground turmeric
1 1/2 tsp cayenne pepper

2 tsp ground cumin
1 tsp fresh ginger, grated
4 garlic cloves, minced
3 onions, chopped
1/3 cup vegetable oil
Salt

- Heat oil in the pan over medium-high heat.
- Add garlic and onions to the pan and sauté for 5 minutes.
- Add turmeric, cayenne, cumin, and ginger and sauté for 1 minute.
- Add broth to the pan and stir well.
- Add meat into the slow cooker with salt.
- Pour pan mixture over the meat.
- Cover and cook on high for 4 hours.
- Just before serving add spinach and cook until wilted, about 5 minutes.
- Add yogurt and stir well.
- Serve and enjoy.

Calories 479, Fat 23 g, Carbohydrates 10.6 g, Sugar 6.4 g, Protein 53.8 g, Cholesterol 157 mg

Classic Lamb Curry

Total Time: 6 hours 15 minutes

Serves: 6

3.3 lbs lamb, diced
2 bay leaves
2 cardamom pods
1 cinnamon stick
1 cup chicken stock
1 tsp red chili powder
1 tsp paprika
1 tsp garam masala
4 tsp ground cumin

4 tsp ground coriander
1 tsp turmeric
6 garlic cloves, crushed
1 tsp ginger, grated
1 large onion, sliced
3 tbsp vegetable oil
1/4 cup all-purpose flour
Salt

- Add flour and lamb into the large zip-lock bag and shake well and set aside.
- Meanwhile, heat 2 tbsp oil in the large frying pan over high heat.
- Add lamb to the pan and cook until browned on both the sides, about 7 minutes.
- Transfer lamb into the slow cooker.
- Heat remaining oil in the pan over medium-high heat.
- Add garlic, ginger, and onion to the pan and sauté for 2 minutes.
- Add turmeric, red chili powder, paprika, garam masala, cumin, and coriander and sauté for 2 minutes.
- Add chicken stock and stir well.
- Transfer pan mixture to the slow cooker.
- Add bay leaves, cardamom, and cinnamon stick.
- Cover and cook on low for 6 hours.
- Serve and enjoy.

Calories 568, Fat 25.7 g, Carbohydrates 8.7 g, Sugar 1.3 g, Protein 71.5 g, Cholesterol 225 mg

Easy Lamb Stew

Total Time: 4 hours 15 minutes

Serves: 4

2 lbs lamb, boneless	2 tsp ground coriander
2 medium onions, chopped	1 tsp ground turmeric
3 garlic cloves, chopped	28 oz can tomatoes, crushed
1 tsp fresh ginger, grated	1.5 tbsp maple syrup
1 tsp dried mint	1 tsp garam masala
2 tbsp vegetable oil	1 tsp red chili flakes
2 tsp ground cumin	2 tsp salt

- Heat oil in the pan over medium heat.
- Add ginger, garlic, and onion to the pan and sauté for 5 minutes.
- Add lamb and cook until browned. Transfer pan mixture into the slow cooker.
- Add remaining ingredients and stir well.
- Cover and cook on high for 4 hours.
- Serve warm and enjoy.

Calories 577, Fat 28.8 g, Carbohydrates 22.2 g, Sugar 13.6 g, Protein 66.5 g, Cholesterol 204 mg

Spicy Beef Roast

Total Time: 5 hours 15 minutes

Serves: 6

2 1/2 lbs beef roast
25 curry leaves
1 tbsp ginger, grated
1 Serrano pepper, minced
2 tbsp lemon juice
2 tbsp garlic, minced
1 tbsp garam masala
1 tsp coriander powder

2 tsp chili powder
1 tsp turmeric
1/2 tsp black pepper
2 onions, chopped
2 tbsp coconut oil
1 tsp mustard seeds
1 tsp salt

- Add all ingredients into the slow cooker and mix well.
- Cover and cook on high for 5 hours.
- Using fork shred the meat and serves.

Calories 421, Fat 16.8 g, Carbohydrates 6.2 g, Sugar 1.9 g, Protein 58.4 g, Cholesterol 169 mg

Spicy Beef Stew

Total Time: 8 hours 25 minutes

Serves: 4

1 lb beef stew meat	1 tsp fresh ginger, chopped
1 cup beef broth	2 garlic cloves, minced
1 onion, sliced	1 tbsp vegetable oil
14.5 oz can tomatoes, diced	Pepper
1 tbsp curry powder	Salt
1 fresh jalapeno pepper, diced	

- Heat oil in the pan over medium heat.
- Add beef to the pan and cook until brown. Transfer to the slow cooker.
- Season browned beef with pepper and salt.
- In same pan, sauté ginger, garlic, and jalapeno for 2 minutes.
- Add tomatoes and curry powder and stir for a minute. Transfer pan mixture to the slow cooker.
- Add remaining ingredients and mix well.
- Cover and cook on low for 8 hours.
- Serve and enjoy.

Calories 293, Fat 11.1 g, Carbohydrates 10 g, Sugar 5 g, Protein 37.2 g, Cholesterol 101 mg

The "Dirty Dozen" and "Clean 15"

Every year, the Environmental Working Group releases a list of the produce with the most pesticide residue (Dirty Dozen) and a list of the ones with the least chance of having residue (Clean 15). It's based on analysis from the U.S. Department of Agriculture Pesticide Data Program report, and unfortunately some popular ingredients in Indian cooking have made the list.

The Environmental Working Group found that 70% of the 48 types of produce tested had residues of at least one type of pesticide. In total there were 178 different pesticides and pesticide breakdown products. This residue can stay on veggies and fruit even after they are washed and peeled. All pesticides are toxic to humans and consuming them can cause damage to the nervous system, reproductive system, cancer, a weakened immune system, and more. Women who are pregnant can expose their unborn children to toxins through their diet, and continued exposure to pesticides can affect their development.

This info can help you choose the best fruits and veggies, as well as which ones you should always try to buy organic.

The Dirty Dozen

Strawberries	Grapes
Spinach	Pears
Nectarines	Cherries
Apples	Tomatoes
Peaches	Sweet bell peppers
Celery	Potatoes

The Clean 15

Sweet corn	Mangoes
Avocados	Eggplant
Pineapples	Honeydew
Cabbage	Kiwi
Onions	Cantaloupe
Frozen sweet peas	Cauliflower
Papayas	Grapefruit
Asparagus	

Measurement Conversion Tables

Volume Equivalents (Liquid)

US Standard	US Standard (ounces)	Metric (Approx.)
2 tablespoons	1 fl oz	30 ml
¼ cup	2 fl oz	60 ml
½ cup	4 fl oz	120 ml
1 cup	8 fl oz	240 ml
1 ½ cups	12 fl oz	355 ml
2 cups or 1 pint	16 fl oz	475 ml
4 cups or 1 quart	32 fl oz	1 L
1 gallon	128 fl oz	4 L

Oven Temperatures

Fahrenheit (F)	Celsius (C) (Approx)
250°F	120°C
300°F	150°C
325°F	165°C
350°F	180°C
375°F	190°C
400°F	200°C
425°F	220°C
450°F	230°C

Volume Equivalents (Dry)

US Standard	Metric (Approx.)
¼ teaspoon	1 ml
½ teaspoon	2 ml
1 teaspoon	5 ml
1 tablespoon	15 ml
¼ cup	59 ml
½ cup	118 ml
1 cup	235 ml

Weight Equivalents

US Standard	Metric (Approx.)
½ ounce	15 g
1 ounce	30 g
2 ounces	60 g
4 ounces	115 g
8 ounces	225 g
12 ounces	340 g
16 ounces or 1 pound	455 g

Recipe Index

Full Index

Want to kick it up a notch?

Double down on healthy living with a full week of fresh, healthy fruit and vegetable juice recipes. A new juice for every day of the week!

Grab this bonus recipe eBook *free* as our gift to you:

http://juice7.hotbooks.org

Made in the USA
Middletown, DE
16 March 2018